The
Forever
Principle

BY Maxine Hancock

Love, Honor and Be Free
Living on Less and Liking It More
People in Process: The Preschool Years

The Forever Principle

MAXINE HANCOCK

FLEMING H. REVELL COMPANY

OLD TAPPAN, NEW JERSEY

Unless otherwise identified, Scripture quotations in this volume are from the King James Version of the Bible.

Scripture quotations identified LB are from The Living Bible, Copyright © 1971 by Tyndale House Publishers, Wheaton, Illinois 60187. All rights reserved.

Scripture quotations identified NAS are from the New American Standard Bible, Copyright © THE LOCKMAN FOUNDATION 1960, 1962, 1963, 1968, 1971, 1973, 1975 and are used by permission.

Scripture quotations identified PHILLIPS are from THE NEW TESTAMENT IN MODERN ENGLISH (Revised Edition), translated by J. B. Phillips. © J. B. Phillips 1958, 1960, 1972. Used by permission of Macmillan Publishing Co., Inc.

Scripture quotations identified RSV are from the Revised Standard Version of the Bible, copyrighted 1946, 1952, © 1971 and 1973.

Excerpt from "Journey of the Magi" by T. S. Eliot reprinted with permission from COLLECTED POEMS 1909–1962, published by Harcourt Brace Jovanovich, Inc.

Library of Congress Cataloging in Publication Data

Hancock, Maxine.
    The forever principle.

    Includes bibliographical references.
    1. Christian life—1960–   2. Commitment
(Psychology)   I. Title.
BV4501.2.H315   248.4   80-12580
ISBN 0-8007-1110-6

To
My husband
Cam
with whom I share the glad bondage
of a truly freeing commitment

Contents

8 Contents

Acknowledgments

My thanks to

> Kathy, who spent another summer with me, typing the early drafts of this book

> Bonnie, a dream-come-true secretary, who has helped me bring the manuscript to completion

> Sharon, who has helped keep the house in order while all this was happening

> Cam, my most severe and most loving critic

> Four children, who have grown in every way, including in an understanding of my ministry of words

We'll have a "Book-End Party" tonight, to celebrate the conclusion of another manuscript. And the One to whom my deepest thanks are due will be a part of that celebration. The book is, after all, because of Him.

MAXINE HANCOCK
February 1979

Preface

This is a book for adults.

Not that it is an "adult book," in the contemporary, salacious sense of the word, in which *adult* is a synonym for licentious, sensual, carnal—the rating on movies, the label on pornographic bookstores, the come-on in mail-order ads.

Nor is it "adult" as the word is used in the sophisticated writing and chatter of the day, where *adult* has become the equivalent of "selfish." In much of today's writing, to be adult seems to mean nothing more or less than being able to do what you want, when you want, how you want, without accountability. The idea of responsibility as a concomitant of adult freedom has been lost. The only person to whom the modern adult feels accountable is himself. The only criterion by which he judges his actions and decisions is his own personal pleasure. A bumper sticker sums up the prevailing philosophy: IF IT FEELS GOOD, DO IT.

In such a cultural setting, it is hard to see how adulthood differs from childhood. The infant is self-focused—tyrannically so. The process of bringing up a child has traditionally involved civilizing him: teaching him, progressively, how to check or mask his persistent and engrossing selfish-

ness. The hope of humanity has been that, eventually, the
world would cease to seem the child's oyster: that as he
matured, the child would be able to consider others at
least as important as himself. But today that concept, too,
has been lost. In *Passages*, Gail Sheehy calls the process of
achieving maturity a "movement from 'us-ness' to 'me-
ness.' "

As "children of a larger growth," self-focused and per-
sistently immature, our generation finds itself unable to
make the commitments that have traditionally helped
make life meaningful. Hence, it should not surprise us that,
amidst a spate of best-selling books on how to assert oneself, how to love oneself, and how to fulfill oneself, we also
have a spate of books taking serious modern readers smack
into blind alleys in pondering the meaning of life.

Discovering meaning in life is the great adult quest. It is
engaging the questions, "What is worth living for?" and
"What is worth dying for?" that truly distinguishes adults
from children. The quest for meaning demands grappling
with the two great problems of human existence—isolation and mortality.

Sadly, today's focus on the self cannot bring satisfactory
meaning to mortality, and it only intensifies the loneliness
and alienation experienced by modern adults. Well educated and well-heeled, today's young adults find themselves
locked into their own selfishness. Isolated from a context of
commitment, even sex has lost its zip. As a generation that
has all but forgotten what William Faulkner called "the old
verities and truths of the heart . . . love and honor and pity
and pride and compassion and sacrifice," many modern

adults live by the dictates "not of the heart, but of the glands."

But personal fulfillment isn't the only area where today's adults are losing out. With an abundance of available information, which would make them the envy of all former generations, many of today's adults lack the ability to make vocational and ethical commitments that would enable them to live with the strength of conviction. Confusing "uncommitted" with "open-minded," they lose the power and courage of conviction—which, historically, has been released for the pursuit of the highest goals of humanity.

Living without a sense of responsibility to God or to others; reading and learning without achieving conviction; committed to no one but self; hopelessly lost in the attempt to break out of personal isolation or to attach meaning to existence, modern adults seem to be only playing at life, like children parading in grown-up clothes. Selfishness, long seen as one of the permanent scars left by the Fall, has now been elevated to a virtue that is necessary for survival in an increasingly junglelike society.

Commitment to others is blocked by commitment to self. Commitment to principle is blocked by commitment to pragmatism: "Whatever works is good." Commitment to eternal values is blocked by commitment to the temporal world. Tied up with self and sense, we have lost sight of transcendent values.

In an age when enormous problems face society, we are experiencing a tragic short-circuiting of adult energies, in endlessly repeating cycles. Energy that could be spent productively is continuously being used to decide who to sleep with, what job to take, what self-help fad to get into. It is my contention that, unless we get serious about making and meaning our commitments, we will be a forgotten, wasted generation, poured out like water on the parched desert of our culture. Only if we find deep channels of commitment, through which to pour our adult energies, will we begin to irrigate this arid social wasteland.

Into the current dialogue on meaning and mortality, on alienation and loneliness, the Christian view of commitment needs to be entered. As a mortal at mid-life, I know there are no easy or pat answers to the great question marks of human existence. But in the face of both ancient and contemporary attempts to answer, I find it exhilarating to affirm meaning and confirm commitment on the basis of the teachings of Scripture. In a day of throw-away commitments, resulting in a perplexed puzzling about the possible meaning of our brief existence, the Christian has some answers to offer the thinking adult, and these answers can only issue in a challenge to learn anew the meaning of making of commitment.

PART I

The Cost and Value of Commitment

What is the value of commitment within human existence? What is its cost? We find commitment to be of inestimable value and immense cost. It is by means of commitment that we discover true personal identity and experience real intimacy. Through commitment, we can find the courage to live creatively and to die confidently. In and through commitment, we experience the central paradox of the Gospel: We lose our lives to find them.

1

Commitment and Identity

May's living room is high ceilinged and rich with dark wood. Around the wainscoted walls hang photographs that link the past to the present, the present to the future. Chiaroscuro portraits from before the days of color photography, they record the cycle of the generations. "That," May says, "is my mother's father. Came from Kentucky, my mother's family did. Yes," with a sigh, "that picture's been with us a long time. She brought it with her when we moved up from Minnesota."

There is a wedding picture: May, tiny beside the tall, young husband. He has been dead for nearly thirty years, now. The picture in the gilt oval frame is of a little child, roundly chubby—May's daughter, at about two. A matching portrait of her son is in the albums stacked in the window seat. On the mantel, there are assorted pictures: wedding photos of grandchildren, school pictures of great-grandchildren.

May is over eighty now. Standing there with her, gazing at those faces to which she is linked by memory and by love, I become aware of how important commitment is.

Continuity

We are young. We are middle-aged. We are old. What
binds it all together? What can make these stages blend,
one into another, as the seasons of the year blend, each a
fulfillment of the previous season? As Kenneth Hamilton
points out, "Truly essential to life is continuity, which is
change with sameness. Life must conserve as well as trans-
form; and change without continuity is wholly destructive."

Next to commitment to God, it is commitment to family
that offers the continuity we need, if we are to integrate
the phases of life. The commitment of marriage, entered
into on a lifelong, non-negotiable basis, allows for that development of continuity accommodating change.

Asked by a student, "What is the significance of marriage in our modern society?" Malcolm Muggeridge replied:

> You young people talk about modern society as if it were
> something other! I see the significance of marriage ex-
> actly as I would have if I had been born many centuries
> ago. It is a *relationship* between a man and a woman. As
> it happens, my own marriage has been exceedingly
> happy; I had my golden wedding anniversary this year.
> When I think of that, and what a lifelong companionship
> like that is worth at the end of one's days, and the joy of
> having children and grandchildren, it overwhelms me.
> To prefer the sort of fugitive or passing fancies for which
> young people today are prepared to sacrifice all their
> lives seems to me absolutely laughable.[1]

The idea of "open marriage," about which so much noise was made a few years ago, has been backtracked on, even by its promulgators. The general consensus now is that commitment, which is exclusive and total, really works much better. "People promoting open marriage," says psychiatrist Sheila Gormely, bluntly, "are in a race for a lonely old age."

Out from the private fountain of marriage flow the other commitments to family, which bind life together and unite it with generations past and those yet to come. The commitment to children certainly brings into focus the meaning of *change with sameness.* I have just dated and filed our children's school pictures, and of one thing I am sure: Family relationships are never—for one year, for one month, even—static. They constitute a continuously adjusting relationship to the dynamic, changing people who are members of the family. And if that's not exciting, I don't know what is. And yet, with all the changes, the persons involved and the basic framework remain the same. And if that's not reassuring, nothing is. In relating to growing, changing children, and then to grandchildren, we have a chance to revisit the brief, vibrant years of childhood. In relating to our aging parents, we have an opportunity to examine and come to terms with growing old.

In love given and love returned, in the cycle of the generations, individual life is offered that thread of continuity that makes it meaningful. The joy of marriage finds its fulfillment in the bearing and rearing of children, so that old age may not be desolation, but rather a feast of ingather-

ing, as the love and commitment made to children is returned.

Cohesion

Commitments ensure continuity in our lives. But another very important element is that of cohesion: bringing
everything together at a center, so life has integrity—
wholeness. And once again, it is commitment that creates
cohesion, bringing together all of life into an orderly de-
sign. Without commitment, the various aspects of life are
disparate and unrelated, like scraps of cloth in a sewing
basket. It is commitment that quilts all those little patches
of living, the bright and the dark, the soft and the harsh,
into a meaningful pattern.

Commitment to a central, controlling life purpose helps
to bring every activity of every day into a meaningful relationship with all other activities. When commitment to
God, through faith in Jesus Christ, has been made a central
focus, all of life comes together at that center, lived in the
light of the one commitment that can transcend time and
link time to eternity.

But commitment is capable not only of centering our
lives, but also of binding our activities within limiting
bounds, so that we do not simply waste energy in fruitless
directions. I often visualize life as a wheel, rolling toward
a life goal (*see* figure 1). Central commitment to God forms
the hub of that wheel, and family and vocational commitments form the outside rim. Various activities become like
spokes of the wheel, radiating out from the center, but

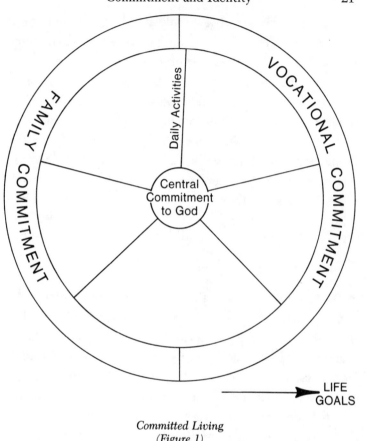

Committed Living
(Figure 1)

bounded by the rim. This saves us from overextension in some directions, and from the go-nowhere experience of being controlled by our activities, instead of by our commitments.

Our commitments shape a life space, within which we can function at peak capacity. Because we are human, we fret at limitations, but it is only within those limitations that we can accomplish anything worthwhile, at the same time keeping life a meaningful, goal-directed whole.

That cohesion gained through commitments is something that orders and lends meaning to life. There is a sense in which every adult choice walls us in, by precluding some other choices. But in the hurry of the past decade to knock down all the walls, we have lost sight of the more satisfying option to accept the walls one has built through commitments and then to decorate them lovingly and live within them creatively.

Coherence

Our commitments to values, to truth, to principles, form a matrix within which we can effect the significant syntheses that make life meaningful. Meaning is not only to be found in goal-directed, cohesive living, but also in focused, clear thinking. We must make judgements as to the value of what we read and hear; we must have standards by which to decide what is right and what is wrong.

The end result of committed and articulate thinking is that we can reject with authority and accept with reason. Jesus was impressive to His hearers because ". . . he taught them as one having authority, and not as the scribes" (Matthew 7:29). While He had that additional sureness of knowing His identity as the One of whom all Scripture spoke, we can share with Him the authority that comes from minds and hearts attuned to God, as He reveals Himself in the Word. In our shaky and unsure age, in which even religious spokesmen are turning East to find answers to life's ultimate questions in Hindu and Buddhist mysticism, the committed Christian thinker can affirm meaning in a material, physical world that comes from the hand of a Creator. He can declare absolute moral values, finding the Law hinging on energetic love for God and unselfish love for one's neighbor. He can live positively under the overarching affirmation, "In the beginning, God . . ." while joining in the fervent whisper, "Even so, come, Lord Jesus."

The final result of this kind of commitment is true personal identity. In commitment, we lose ourselves. In continuity and cohesion, we find ourselves. Coherently, then, we can speak to our generation.[2]

The extreme fragmentation of life, in which adults have come to think that no structure can last longer than seven or eight years, has resulted in a generation haunted by the question of identity: "Who am I?"

I walked across our pasture quarter with a Christian woman of mature years. "I've asked lots of questions," she said, "and had lots of doubts. But I have never wondered who I was. I have always known that. If the intellectuals of today are really unsure of their identities, if they are really asking, 'Who am I?' then what it means to be *lost* takes on a new and terrifying meaning."

Soren Kierkegaard pointed out, "the realization of an authentic self is possible for an individual only if he enters into a relationship with God by faith." True identity is created, affirmed, and mirrored in commitments. By means of them, life ceases to be the patches of a fool's motley and becomes, instead, a seamless robe.

2

Commitment and Intimacy

... If any one wishes to come after Me, let him
deny himself, and take up his cross, and follow Me.
For whoever wishes to save his life shall lose it; but
whoever loses his life for My sake shall find it.

—Matthew 16:24, 25 NAS

We were strangers, meeting as travelers do, spending an
hour together and then vanishing from each other's lives.
But I can't forget her. An executive with a multinational
corporation, she was on her way to a business meeting. She
epitomized contemporary womanhood: well educated,
very much in charge of herself, and newly divorced. As she
discovered that I combined family commitments with a
writing career, she raised the question: "How do you keep
it all together?"

I explained to her that I had a few non-negotiable commitments that framed my life. "First," I told her, shaping
my left hand into a half-circle, "I have a commitment to
Jesus Christ as Lord and Saviour, and to the authority of
His Word over my life. And secondly," I shaped my right
hand to complete the circular frame, "I have a commit-

ment to my husband and my four children that, in 'doing my thing,' I in no way hinder their full development as persons, as well."

She looked at the framework I had shaped.

"You see," I said, "within those commitments, I have a clearly defined space of very real personal freedom."

She listened intently, thoughtfully. "Do you mean," she asked finally, her voice reflecting mild incredulity, "that you put commitment to *others* ahead of commitment to *yourself?*"

In her question I heard the bewilderment of our whole generation. We have been advised from all sides that the most important commitment of life is to ourselves. And when we find that commitment to be empty, lonely, and unrewarding, we don't really know where to turn. The idea that one could find meaning in life through commitments outside of himself—so long a principle in all that is noblest and best in the human story—has almost been lost. We need, desperately, to have it restated and reaffirmed.

As human adults, we are not only caught in the vortex of the closing circle of morality, but also in the isolation of the closed circle of our own individualism. The isolation and alienation of the individual has a history that goes back to the moment of the Fall in the Garden of Eden. Cut off from fellowship with God, Adam and Eve also found themselves alienated from each other. In the next generation, a bitter sibling rivalry found its consummation in fratricide. The alienation of man from man had become so great that it would be reflected down through the ages, in history and literature and drama.

As modern man has become more and more concerned about the self, he has moved toward increasing isolation of the person. Lonely people are the theme of our popular songs and a central issue in the arts and social sciences, for the ancient modes of transcending isolation are being lost. In a society that lacks a positive evaluation of commitment, it is not surprising that people are lonely, cut off, locked into themselves, listening in vast numbers to the sounds of silence.

At a graduation ceremony, I recently heard a young psychologist offer advice to those who were graduating. "The best advice I can give you is 'know thyself,' " he said. He was a voice of our age. The best advice that seems to be available is to "get in touch with yourself." To a world of trapped, isolated people, suffering in the closed circles of their individual existences, the wisdom of today offers just more of self. It is tragically like calling in the arsonist to put out the fire.

The Greeks saw it more clearly, perhaps. Sophocles' *Oedipus Rex* is a classical exposition of alienation. As Oedipus is progressively united to himself in knowledge of his parentage, his past, and his moral guilt, he is at the same time and by the same knowledge progressively alienated from his society, his position, his family. The tragedy of *Oedipus Rex* is the humanistic tragedy. We have adopted from the Greeks an absorption with self-knowledge. But we have failed to learn from them that making self the goal of knowledge can lead only to isolation, alienation, and despair.

As long as we espouse knowledge of the self as the goal

of learning, we will continue to lock ourselves into the closed circles of despair. All of us find that "the indiscernible track of ancient guilt" leads to our own doorsteps. The prophetic finger points to each of us, as to Oedipus: "You are the godless defiler of this land." What we learn from honest self-analysis is that ". . . all have sinned, and come short of the glory of God" (Romans 3:23). Self-knowledge leads us only to a knowledge of our fallen state, no matter how artfully we attempt to explain it away.

Clearly, we must learn something more than our own sinful condition, if ever we are to find a way out of the closed circle of alienation from God and from others. Contrasted with the humanistic goals of knowledge are the biblical goals. The knowledge of good and of evil was prohibited to Adam and Eve, for they were to have a higher concern—the knowledge of the holy.

A young Swede shared our breakfast table with us one summer while he worked for us. One morning, after Cam had read from Proverbs, he summoned enough English to ask, "What does it mean—'The fear of the Lord is the beginning of knowledge?' It was written up across the front of the classroom when I went to school, and I never could understand it."

What does it mean? We wrestled with that question for days and wrestle with it still. It means at least that if we can get a glimpse of the Holy One, if we can understand something of His justice and holiness, we can begin to interpret our sinfulness against the backdrop of reality. Generally speaking, nobody is much abashed to admit that he is a sinner, with a hasty caveat: "But no worse than anyone else I know, and not as bad as some." But our sin is first *against* God and only secondarily *before* man. That is how Joseph understood it when he refused the seductive offers of Potiphar's wife: ". . . how then can I do this great wickedness, and sin against God?" (Genesis 39:9). And that is how, when he had come to himself, the prodigal son at last understood the seriousness of his sin: ". . . I have sinned against heaven, and before thee" (Luke 15:18).

Only in the light of the knowledge of God's holiness and our sinfulness can we begin to appreciate His love and the outflowing of His grace in Jesus Christ. And only then can we regain the confidence, as forgiven persons, to enter into real relationships—first to God, and then to each other.

The Old Testament prophets point out that the future hope of man lies in a day when the knowledge of the Lord shall cover the earth as the waters cover the sea (*see* Isaiah 11:9). Meanwhile, we need to heed the words of such contemporary prophets as J. I. Packer, foreign as they may sound to ears so accustomed to the know-thyself doctrine:

> What were we made for? To know God. What aim should we set ourselves in life? To know God. What is the "eternal life" that Jesus gives? Knowledge of God. "This is life eternal, that they might know thee, the only true God, and Jesus Christ, whom thou hast sent" (John 17:3). What is the best thing in life, bringing more joy, delight, and contentment, than anything else? Knowledge of God. . . . What makes life worth while is having a big enough objective, something which catches our imagination and lays hold of our allegiance; and this the Christian has. . . . For what higher, more exalted, and more compelling goal can there be than to know God?[3]

As we come to know God and make commitment of our life to Him through faith in Jesus Christ, the underlying problems of guilt and selfishness, which cut us off from one another, are also dealt with. We acknowledge our sinfulness and accept full pardon on the basis of Christ's sacrifice at Calvary. And then, in the acceptance we find, we are set free. We can say, "Oh, God, You have made a way by which You can be 'just and justifier' at once. And when I put my trust in Your Son as Lord and Saviour, You declare me to be 'accepted in the beloved.' "

Suddenly I find that I no longer need to protect, defend, barricade myself within the stone circle of self. I can let down the drawbridge, open the windows, fly the flag of joy from the turret, as I open myself to loving, to living, to giving.

Not through knowledge of ourselves, but through the knowledge of God, do we find our way out of the loneliness of individualism. Set free in this way, we can learn in a whole new way the meaning of commitment—commitment first to God, and then to others—which really liberates.

Erik Erikson sees the most important stage of development in adulthood to be "the crisis of intimacy." Bruno Bettelheim states that the familiar fairy-tale ending of prince and princess living happily ever after "does indicate that which alone can take the sting out of the narrow limits of our time on this earth: forming a truly satisfying bond to another."[4] Commitment is the way to break out of our shells of isolation.

The paradox of commitment is seen everywhere. One

must let go of life, in order to truly receive life. One must forget self, in order to find self. And only through self-forgetful self-finding can we truly give ourselves to others— and make life meaningful by relationships that are intimate, lasting, and satisfying.

3

Commitment and the Courage to Live

> Moderation in the feelings of fear and confidence is
> courage . . . he that exceeds in confidence is fool-
> hardy, while he that exceeds in fear but is deficient
> in confidence is cowardly.
>
> —Aristotle

The lead character of a striking feminist novel of the six-
ties, *The Edge*, by Shirley Mezvinsky, defines life symboli-
cally as a lion that must be controlled by a tamer with a
strong stick and an air of sureness and authority. Individuals who cannot fearlessly command the lion are devoured
by it. Unfortunately, Lois Marks finds her stick not stout
enough, or her confidence great enough to handle the lion
of life. She commits suicide. Her retreat from life is the
story of thousands of our generation who, through perhaps
less drastic measures, cease from encountering the challenge of meaningful living.

Living without commitments that bind life to meanings
greater than self, many find themselves unable to cope with
life. The fact that suicide ranks as the second-highest cause
of death for people between the ages of fifteen and forty

tells part of the story of our sad retreat from life; increasing alcoholism and drug dependency tell of other escape routes. Without commitments, we are entirely vulnerable to the devouring lions of life.

Living Tenaciously

Living tenaciously, surviving and desiring to survive, has become a challenge in our day. Most of us are not content to merely survive. We want to live creatively or, at least, constructively. But there are situations when just living demands the greatest of courage. Nobody has detailed such circumstances more graphically than has Aleksandr Solzhenitsyn. In the dark pages of *The Gulag Archipelago*, the only bright strands are the stories of people whose commitments kept them human, in spite of the degradation of slave-labor camps. His story of the vibrant Christian witness of Vera Korneyeva, for example, reveals how courage for living in the face of death is generated by commitments that reach beyond death.

In his study of life in the death camps, Terrence Des Pres points out that the survivor is a person who commits himself to endure, in order to be able to tell the story of the prison experience. This "Will to Bear Witness" impels him to survive.

Many of the survivors willed to tell the story of "man's inhumanity to man." Others lived to tell of the death of their faith. Corrie ten Boom willed to tell the world another message: "There is no pit so deep but what His love is deeper still."

Reflecting on the lessons of the Holocaust, Helmut Thielicke comments that:

> ... the uncommitted mind ... all too easily succumbs to the law of least resistance. The person who insists upon maintaining his self-respect in the midst of the terror or refusing to become an object of contempt in the face of the hunger and dread of a concentration camp does not need to be an "educated" man; but he must have inner reserves and commitments. The best and most reliable "resisters" were to be found among mature Christians—not among those who merely went along with the Christian convention—and among Communists. . . .[5]

Solzhenitsyn says, "The old women are bolder than the rest. You couldn't turn them bad. They believe in God."

Living Confessionally

In the less extreme but still challenging circumstances of normal life, the Christian's courage to live is, simply, the courage to confess. He does not cling to life because he is afraid to die, but because he has a deep desire to fulfill the tasks entrusted to him. He wants not merely to live, but to live confessionally.

Living morally is a confession of commitment to the principle of accountability. I think of a young woman who was engaged to a newly graduated lawyer. Soon after their engagement, he suggested that they might as well live together, since they were planning to marry, anyhow. "No way," the girl responded. "When we're married, we'll live together—and not before." She stood her ground. He broke the engagement and her heart.

I think of another young woman. Committed in a marriage that was everything but happy, she met a single man who answered to many of her shattered ideals, including her need for spiritual understanding. But both she and her friend were committed to living life, first of all, as an act of confession to their faith in Jesus Christ as Lord. They made a decision, and a tough one: They stopped seeing each other.

"Fools," cry the voices of our day, "to pass up a chance for happiness!" In a day when all of society urges personal happiness as the only measure of right and wrong, these young people exemplify courage: Courage born of a commitment to live lives pleasing to God, courage to put that commitment ahead of any personal fulfillment.

Living confessionally demands standing alone against the crowd—even, most often, the crowd of Christians. Jesus warned that the gate was narrow and the way "strait," and despite the highway-widening projects of many modern presentations of the Gospel, still "few there be that find it" (*see* Luke 13:24).

In our current Western society, the courage we need is to live ". . . blameless and harmless, the sons of God, without rebuke, in the midst of a crooked and perverse nation . . ." (Philippians 2:15). In other times and in other settings, Christians have needed the courage to make their confession under much greater pressure.

The courage to confess is often made of a thousand tiny decisions—none heroic in itself. I was moved by an article in *Christianity Today* in which the simple resistance of one family against Hitler was recounted. Nothing big: just day-to-day living under the authority of God, choosing His laws over Hitler's where they were in conflict. In the face of the tragic failure of the Church as a whole to take a stand against Hitler, how glad I am to read the record of the small heroisms of personal courage.

Even in our free society, the Christian who lives in true confession needs something more than bumper-sticker witness. He, too, needs the courage to create his witness from the day-to-day decisions of everyday life.

Living Creatively

Living within commitment is not only the source of courage for tenacious and confessional living, but also the source of courage for creative living. It is strange that, in a day that honors creativity high on its list of values, the energy needed for creative, constructive living is being wasted in repeated cycles of selecting a mate and a career.

But I am encouraged to find that thinking young people today are stumbling onto the value of commitment, many of them encountering it with surprise. I remember talking with a woman in her early thirties, who had wrestled for a number of years with the temptation to call it quits in her marriage. Certainly, her marriage was not of the made-in-heaven variety. But finally she decided that she was not going to get out. She was going to go through. "I think if we can make our marriage last," she told me, "anybody can."

At the moment of that decision, the cost seemed immense. And yet, when the inner turmoil of reaching the

decision had subsided, she suddenly discovered herself
with new energy, new decisiveness. She made plans for
dovetailing her renewed family commitments with further
education plans. She began to see—and use—the advan-
tages of her circumstances. "It's a funny thing," she said,
"but now that I've gotten the marriage thing settled, I
have energy for other things in life. I spent all my creative
energy, for the past few years, just rebelling against my situation!"

She spoke for those who today are coming back to a realization of the basic values of commitment. The discovery
is being reflected in magazine articles and novels. But we
would have to look a long way to find it put any better
than by Leo Tolstoy. In *Anna Karenina,* he explores the
gradual deterioration of meaning in the lives of Anna and
Vronsky, as they pursue an adulterous relationship, heed-
less of prior commitments. Almost at dead center of this
great novel, Anna's lover is given a piece of advice by his
friend:

> There's only one way of having love conveniently with-
> out its being a hindrance—that's marriage. How, how am
> I to tell you what I mean? . . . Wait a minute, wait a min-
> ute! Yes . . . you can only carry a load and do something
> with your hands when the load is tied on your back, and
> that's marriage. And that's what I felt when I was mar-
> ried. My hands were suddenly set free. But to drag that
> load about you without marriage, your hands will always
> be so full that you can do nothing.[6]

In commitment, some things are settled, made an integral part of life, resolved with finality; the hands are free to make, to do, to serve.

Not only does commitment release energy for creative service, it also provides a life structure in which there is both order and limit. Although we can all conjure the mental image of the artist as a wild-haired, frenzied eccentric, living without order, limits, or commitment, history shows that much of the best of art has been done within lives framed by personal commitment. The music of Bach, the poetry of Browning, the prose of Dickens, all argue for the possibility of creative flowering within the limitations of commitment. In *The Courage to Create*, Rollo May makes the statement, *"Creativity itself requires limits*, for the creative act arises out of the struggle of human beings with and against that which limits them."

Limitations in the form of commitments allow for the focusing of creative potential. As the magnifying glass catches the diffuse rays of the sun and focuses them on a small point to create fire, so the limitations of life can bring together our creative abilities, narrow the ways in which they can be used, and focus activity on one burning point.

While personal commitment releases energy and provides a framework for creating, transcendent commitment provides a purpose for creating. The creative act, making new arrangements from existing components, is a demanding, exhausting undertaking. There must be a motivation to create that is so compelling it cannot be ignored. The

Christian, living confessionally, has such a compelling commitment: to live and to create in such a way that God is glorified. In viewing our lives and our work as mirror surfaces, reflecting God's goodness to mankind and His glory back to Him, the desire to polish and refine the reflecting surface is strong. Within the framework of a Christian commitment, the discipline of creativity has a purpose. Our best is all that is good enough to offer to God.

Creativity is, of course, impossible without the discipline that binds craftsmanship to spontaneity. I had a conversation not long ago with a young man who is a spontaneous balladeer. He had strummed his way from hostel to hostel for a number of years, singing and playing his guitar. Now, as a new Christian, he had a problem. "My songs don't feel good," he told me. "They're rough. If I'm singing for God, they have to be better than they are."

"How do you write?" I asked.

He shrugged. "The song just comes," he said, "and I play it."

"How do you rewrite?"

"What? I never rewrite. I'm always afraid I'll ruin something."

We talked together, then, about the necessity of crafting: the spontaneity of idea, linked with the painstaking skills of composition. He went home to rework a recent composition. His commitment to Christ compelled him to subject himself to a rigorous discipline.

Living creatively requires the courage to accept rejection, repudiation, and the disappointment of bumping up against one's own limitations. But commitment can provide both the courage and the intensity of passion that are necessary to constructive productivity.

In the National Art Gallery in Washington, I found myself fighting tears as I stood before the great Rembrandt canvasses. In those paintings, I read the creative witness of a fellow believer of three centuries earlier. I had the same feeling then—a feeling of desolation at my own inability, yet of exultation at the glory of artistic endeavor done for the glory of God—that sweeps over me when I read Dostoevsky or listen to Bach.

For the committed Christian, the courage to create does not spring from his desire to defy death, but from his urgency to declare death conquered and from his commitment to its Conqueror. We live in an age that is crying for a fresh outburst of Christian creativity, on the grand scale, as well as in the private acts of creativity in home and family life. It is from the strength of irrevocable commitments to God and to others that the ability to live tenaciously, confessionally, creatively, can spring. Then the Christian can join in the triumphant cry of the Apostle Paul: "For to me to live is Christ, and to die is gain" (Philippians 1:21).

4

Commitment and the Courage to Die

It was a funny trip across the continent. An earlier flight had been canceled, and the plane was crammed. I found myself between two professors returning from a convention. One was calmly reading Ernest Becker's *The Denial of Death.* The other sat down, mopped his brow, and took what he told me was his third tranquillizer that afternoon. Obviously, for him, flying was a hand-to-hand wrestle with the Death Angel. I sat between them. I had to evaluate. How did my commitments make my attitudes different from the professor on my left, who professed a cool and stoic acceptance of death, and the one on my right, who flew in fear?

I don't like the idea of death. I get thoroughly impatient with those who talk about death as a friend to greet, or as a "stage of growth." Death, the Bible tells us, is an enemy. It is the last enemy that will be destroyed. But it has lost its power to warp and distort life by constant fear, for the Christian who joins in the triumphant shout: ". . . Death is swallowed up in victory. O death, where is thy sting? O grave, where is thy victory?" (1 Corinthians 15:54, 55.)

It is the Christian who dares to live openly conscious of death. As Annie Dillard states in an interview:

> Agnostics often think that people run to God because they are afraid of dying. On the contrary ... people in the Bible understood the transitory nature—the risk—of life better than most people. They aren't using religion as an escape hatch. Faith forces you to a constant awareness of final things. Agnostics don't remember all the time that they're going to die. But Christians do remember.[7]

The Christian is aware of an eternal dimension and sees that dimension in sharp juxtaposition with everyday life. The "now" and "then" are separated only by the heavy, black line that is death.

I grew up under a wall motto familiar to anyone who shares my background: ONLY ONE LIFE, 'TWILL SOON BE PAST. ONLY WHAT'S DONE FOR CHRIST WILL LAST. In those incredibly long days of childhood, I heard my mother sing softly:

> Life at best is very brief,
> Like the falling of a leaf,
> Or the binding of a sheaf,
> Be in time.

I loved to hear my mother sing, and I especially liked the rhyme of this particular song. But I thought the words absurd. Life brief?—when it was still two hours till supper time? The only time life was brief in those days was just before bedtime. And, of course, that is the experience of life. Life gets briefer as death becomes more clearly inevitable.

In *Denial of Death,* Ernest Becker sees religious faith as the best hope for both acknowledging the reality of death and yet living beyond it. "The irony of man's condition is that the deepest need is to be free of the anxiety of death and annihilation; but it is life itself which awakens it, and so we must shrink from being fully alive," he says early in his book. After reviewing the contributions of Kierkegaard, Freud, and Rank to the discussion of mortality, Becker concludes, "Religion solves the problem of death . . . [it] gives the possibility of heroic victory in freedom and solves the problem of human dignity at its highest level."

A recent attempt to tackle the dark subject of perishability without a religious orientation is Gail Sheehy's *Passages.* I was coming up to my thirty-fifth birthday when I took time to read this influential book. Since I was the same age as Sheehy had been when she narrowly missed death in a terrorist shoot-out and thus became aware of her own mortality, I could identify strongly with her.

Furthermore, I had had my own head-on confrontation with mortality just two years earlier. Ill with an undiagnosed condition, I had lain in a hospital bed, wracked with pain and experiencing progressive paralysis in a nightlong encounter with death. I had attempted my own diagnosis through a fog of sedation. I was having a stroke or a heart attack. And then, as my head exploded and contracted and my limbs numbed and contorted, I found myself struggling for each successive breath. This was not just a heart attack or a stroke, I concluded. It was death. Not quite thirty-three, I was dying.

In the several hours in which I confronted mortality that night, I came to some very different conclusions from those of Gail Sheehy. Sheehy's breakthrough discovery was, "No one is with me. No one can keep me safe. There is no one who won't ever leave me alone."

I found, on the other hand, that I could fully agree—not just intellectually, but by experience—with the Psalmist: "Yea, though I walk through the valley of the shadow of death, I will fear no evil: for thou art with me. . . ." Facing death at thirty-three, I learned—with the luminosity of personal experience—that for one whose life and future rests with Jesus Christ as Saviour and Lord, death's shadow is indeed illumined by the glorious presence of the One who has tasted death for us.

Against such a background of personal experience, I could only be fascinated by Sheehy's book, which explores ways in which adults cope with the fear of death. "The thought of death is too terrifying to confront head-on," Sheehy states. She suggests three strategies by which adults attempt to cope with their death fears. She finds these to be analogous to what a frightened child in a dark room might do: "switch on the lights," or acquire knowledge; "call for help," or look for a Strong One; ignore the fear by keeping busy with other thoughts. The author opts for the first technique. She tries to turn on the lights.

Facing the same fearful confrontation, the Christian opts for the second alternative. We call for help to One who has promised, "I will never leave thee nor forsake

thee." We face our fear of death on the arm of the Strong
One. This does not mean, of course, that we cannot em-
pathize with the struggle of others to "turn on the lights."

Certainly, believers and nonbelievers alike share the
sense of imminent mortality, of being bound in fast-run-
ning, relentless, and limited time. Moving across the great
divide, into the second half of our short term here on earth
about age thirty-five, is almost certain to signal a crisis of
varying dimensions. Most people in this stage of life go
through a period of re-evaluation, of casting aside youth-
ful illusions, of setting new and more realistic goals. In
Thoreau's words, "The youth gets together his materials to
build a bridge to the moon, or perchance, a palace or tem-
ple on earth, and, at length, the middle-aged man concludes to build a woodshed of them." For the Christian,
this complex time of sorting out goals and priorities is conducted not only in light of the shortness of life, but also in
view of the values of eternity.

But beyond the bondage to time we all share, *Passages*
documents only bondages of the human spirit. Written as
it is from a purely human perspective, without any sense of
the redeeming work of Christ, the book describes the
human condition since the flaming sword blocked a return
to Eden. *Passages* is a footnote to *Paradise Lost*—a study of
human bondage.

The writer reveals the bondage to self and the illusory
freedom that is really bondage to sin. The pace-setter
group, whose case studies are cited, lives without the
"bondage" of conventional morality. It is a group that
thereby lives in pathetic bondage to sin. The "mature

married man," who dissolves his home and business to
chase nymphs down the California coast, rates more pity
than approbation. Women who indulge in "random and
meaningless affairs" are equally pathetic.

The ultimate bondage, however, about which this book
is written—and out of which it is written—is bondage to
the fear of death. Releasing mankind from that bondage is
cited by the writer of the Hebrews as the prime cause for
Christ's Incarnation, death, and victorious resurrection:

> ... he also became a human being, so that by going
> through death as a man he might destroy him who had
> the power of death, that is, the devil; and might also set
> free those who lived their whole lives a prey to the fear of
> death.
>
> Hebrews 2:14, 15 PHILLIPS

The full extent of the bondage of the fear of death is doc-
umented by *Passages.* It is fear of death, "something alien,
horrible, unspeakable but undeniable—my own death,"
which drives Sheehy to a personal breakdown, and in turn,
to her research. And from that bondage, Sheehy can offer
no escape. She ends the book as she begins it, bound by
fear of death. "Turning on the lights" has only revealed
that she has many companions in the house of bondage.

It takes something more than mere acknowledgement of
death, something more than even charting its phases, to
deliver us from the fear of death. It takes Someone who has
been there, and who promises to be with us; Someone who
has met death and defeated it; Someone to whom we have

committed our lives and to whom we can safely commit ourselves in dying.

What, specifically, do we fear in death?

First, I think we fear being alone, cut off from our loved ones. I know I had to work through that fear the night I faced death. A haunting aloneness swept over me, as I pictured my parents and my husband coming in the next morning to find me—gone. And this fear stayed with me, until I became assured that beyond death I would be united with Him to whom my deepest commitments were made, united with all the family of God who had died before me, and eventually reunited with all of my loved ones who also made commitments to Jesus Christ. It was the presence of Christ Himself, made very real to me in those dark hours, that made me realize the absolute truth of His promise, "I will never leave thee, nor forsake thee."

Then, I think we are afraid of being cut off from our life work. I remember, that night, arguing intensely with God: "Lord, I've done only a little writing for You." A shiny new copy of my recently published first book sat on the windowsill of my hospital room. "If You let me live, I'll go on writing for You." Gradually, my mind was suffused with the illumination that, if I were to die, it would not be the end of my vocation, but only the beginning. All that I would ever do on this side of death would amount to nothing more than the scribbles in a student's copybook, just practicing for an eternity of glad service.

As we think of death, we are harrowed, too, with a fear of pain. "Oh joy, oh delight, should we go without dying. No sickness, no sadness, no dreading, no crying!" How beautifully the old hymn expresses the hope of being caught up to be with the Lord—a transition to eternity that one generation of the Church will indeed know. But in the meanwhile, we hope for something swift and relatively painless, while watching, numb with aching, as people we love suffer. In a culture oriented to comfort and to pleasure, the very idea of pain and discomfort is appalling. And yet, once again, we find that Christ holds out His hands to comfort. For He has taken the cup of human suffering and drunk it to the bottom. And in pain, we find Him there to sustain. The "fellowship of his sufferings" is something unknown to those who have not suffered, but it is a deep and sweet communion, known to those who have experienced pain and found that, at its worst, pain has opened out into communion. The blood He shed was for our sins, to bring about atonement. But the broken body was His total experience of our human suffering and pain. Once again, what we fear becomes something beautiful when illumined by the Presence of Our Lord.

Another element in the fear of death is the fear of dissolution, the horror of ceasing to be. We are so intensely aware of ourselves, a knit-together person of body, soul, and spirit. How can we face not being? It is only orthodox Christian doctrine, which sees the resurrection and reuniting of the whole person—body and soul and spirit—which tells us that beyond this dissolution is a new existence, that "this mortality must put on immortality." The resurrected flesh-and-bones body of Jesus Christ, recognizable, tangible, tells us that in our glorified state we will be whole— whole with a wholeness we only approximate in our short, earthly existence; whole for all eternity. What a glad hope in our calling! "Beloved, now are we the sons of God, and it doth not yet appear what we shall be: but we know that, when he shall appear, we shall be like him; for we shall see him as he is" (1 John 3:2).

There is still one fear of death. It is, perhaps, the greatest. Distasteful as the idea of nonexistence is to sentient creatures, even more fearful is the ". . . dread of something after death, That undiscover'd country from whose bourn no traveller returns. . . ."[8] Written in our hearts is the truth that, ". . . it is appointed unto men once to die, but after this the judgement" (Hebrews 9:27). There is both terror and hope in this truth. It is a truth which, once embraced with all its soul-searching implications, sets us free.

Solzhenitsyn chronicles the story of a little old woman being interrogated for her assistance to a church official. Despite the menace of fist-shaking jailers, she replied, "There is nothing you can do with me even if you cut me into pieces. After all, you are afraid of your bosses and you are afraid of each other . . . but I am not afraid of anything. I would be glad to be judged by God right this minute."[9]

The assurance of Christ's presence in the dark valley; of His fellowship in suffering; of ultimate wholeness and reunion with those with love in eternal, unending life of service to Our Lord; and of an ultimate righteous judgment, can give the Christian courage to live life fully and face death triumphantly.

It was a long flight, that afternoon. As the continent folded and flattened and crumpled beneath us, the professor on my right discussed *Denial of Death* with me. I shared with him my view that by Christ's resurrection, death's hold has been broken, and hence the Christian does not need either to deny it or to acquiesce to it. The other professor—the nervous one—seemed gradually to relax. I thought probably the tranquillizers had finally taken hold.

But near the end of the trip, he turned to me. "You have been a great help to me," he said. I was surprised, because we hadn't really talked together. "Ordinarily, I would have taken several more pills and this." He pulled out a little flask of whiskey. "But today I didn't need them. You somehow seem so calm, so at peace, that you gave me good vibrations. I decided I had better remember what I learned, growing up as a Presbyterian, about trusting God."

The Christian can hate death as God hates it. But he need not fear it, deny it, or pretend to accept it. He can face it, sharing God's anger at it, yet confident that "... to be absent from the body" is "to be present with the Lord" (*see* 1 Corinthians 5:3). And this gives him confidence to live, to die—even to fly!

5

The Cost of Commitment

Whatever is worthwhile in this short life requires that we pay the cost of commitment. If we are to know more than selfishness, to reach out of our closed circle of self to experience true intimacy, then there must be costly commitment: commitment that involves denying ourselves some fleeting pleasures for the privilege of sharing life with one partner. If we are to have serious and significant vocation, then we must make commitment that precludes many other interesting possibilities. If we are able to know union with God, then we must make the costly commitment of discipleship to Jesus Christ as Lord, a commitment that requires us to "sell all . . . and follow."

To live as a committed individual is to live as costly ointment, poured out in worship and love. It is only when commitment is costly that it is of value. To suggest that one can experience salvation without first signing away his life to God is to offer "cheap grace." To suggest that one can experience the joy of real marriage without subordinating oneself to the union is to offer something less than becoming "one flesh."

From Fantasy to Reality

All commitment is costly, because it invites us into a new relationship to reality. In our hedonistic age, with DO IT! stickers plastered on lockers in high-school corridors, we are assailed with invitations to immediate gratification. The idea of postponing sex until after marriage, in order to build a lasting love on a foundation of trust, is so foreign as to be nearly incomprehensible to many. Commitment invites us out of the narrow, little world of "here and now," "me, myself, and I," and "feeling," into a larger reality of eternal values, an orientation toward others, and the eternal facts that supersede feeling. And all such invitations require a costly reordering of our view of real values. We have to be able to distinguish between the false felicity of wealth, respect, power, and fame and the true happiness of being in harmony with God. Then, with Boethius, we can cry:

> Disperse the clouds of earthly matter's cloying weight;
> Shine out in all Thy glory; for Thou art rest and peace . . .
> To see Thee is our end,
> Who art our source and maker, lord and path and goal.

All of this rethinking will be costly. "I don't think that my husband will ever become a Christian," a wife told me sadly. "He has never been able to give up one thing to secure another." And all like him are doomed . . . not only later, but now.

From Paganism to True Worship

Not only do we have to abandon false notions of happiness and redirect our lives toward true happiness, to make real commitment. We also have to abandon the idols of our pagan age. Rollo May points out that the ". . . saint must fight the actual . . . gods of our society—the god of conformism as well as the gods of apathy, material success, and exploitative power. These are the 'idols' of our society that are worshipped by multitudes of people."[10] To enter into true commitment is also, as Kenneth Hamilton so ably points out, to cease to do obeisance to "the Great God Change." For, as Jesus made very clear, "No man can serve two masters." The God of the New Testament, no less than the God of the Old, demands wholehearted, singleminded commitment and worship.

All of this requires that we pay the cost of being a peculiar people. And that is costly, for "contempt is the chief weapon the worshippers of the Great God Change use against traditional Christianity."[11] Learning to live confidently amidst contempt has always been the task of the committed Christian. But it is not only the contempt he faces because he dares to think in different modes that makes commitment costly, but also the personal cost of being out of the community with most of the thinkers of his age. In T. S. Eliot's "Journey of the Magi," the narrator speaks of the utter change of life brought about by the worship of the Christ child. He concludes:

> We return to our places, these Kingdoms,
> But no longer at ease here, in the old dispensation,
> With an alien people clutching their gods.
> I should be glad of another death.

"No longer at ease here" certainly summarizes the Christian experience. Learning to pay the cost of commit-

ment means learning—with Abraham, Isaac, and Jacob—
what it means to live as pilgrims and strangers.

Commitment costs, too, because one commitment is exclusive of many others. Having made one choice, many
other choices are automatically ruled out. Elizabeth
O'Connor points out, in *Eighth Day of Creation:*

> If I develop one gift, it means that other gifts will not be
> used. Doors will close on a million lovely possibilities. I
> will become a painter or a doctor only if denial becomes
> a part of my picture of reality. Commitment at the point
> of my gifts means that I must give up being a straddler.
> Somewhere in the deeps of me I know this. Life will not
> be the smorgasbord I have made it, sampling and tasting
> here and there. . . . But I do not like the sound of this. I do
> not want to be boxed in.

Edith Schaeffer tells of a young man with whom she had
conversation concerning becoming a Christian. Finally he
said, "My questions are answered—but how can I bow? . . .
I want not only to go on in an interesting life of my own
will, but I want to continue comparing one teaching and
another. I enjoy the search. If I bow, that freedom will be
over."[12]

Perhaps the most moving contemporary story of the cost
of commitment is one I heard Madame Georges Vanier re-
count in a television interview. After the death of her husband, a former Governor General of Canada, Madame
Vanier entered a convent for a period of spiritual retreat.
The speaker at the retreat one morning gave a message on

the rich young ruler. Madame Vanier went back to her room, deeply troubled, for like the young ruler, she was rich. She had a luxurious home, an adoring family—and an open invitation from her son Jean to join him in his work with retarded adults in France. She spent the day in tears, then went to the Mother Superior of the convent, to announce her commitment. Knowing full well the cost, she renounced the comforts of her luxurious Canadian home, to join in Jean's work of caring at L'Arche.

From Rebellion to Surrender

But the cost of commitment is more than merely the cost of being "peculiar" in our generation, and more, even, than denying oneself a thousand tempting byways in the pursuit of the Way. Truly spiritual commitment touches at the very heart of the human condition. The posture of worship, which is essential to commitment, is most difficult. We have come to admire the man who stands on his own two feet and shakes his fist in the direction of heaven, crying, "I am the master of my fate: I am the captain of my soul."[13]

Yet this stance of man in rebellion against his Maker is the central tragedy of the human condition. It is only in capitulation to the King of creation, God Himself, that the rebel human heart can ever find any real rest or sense of meaning. This paradox is expressed in John Donne's *Sonnet XIV:*

> Take mee to you, imprison mee, for I
> Except you 'enthrall mee, never shall be free,
> Nor even chast, except you ravish mee.

The word *commitment* is somewhat misleading, when we talk about entering into a relationship of fellowship with God. The word *surrender* is, I think, closer to what is required of us, for mankind is basically in rebellion against God. We need to surrender in the sense that, as rebels against God, we lay down our arms and accept His sovereignty and control in our lives. How difficult it is for each of us, sharing in the central human sin of pride, to come to this point of surrender. Like computer billings, we do not want to be bent or folded—especially at the knees. C. S. Lewis, in *Surprised by Joy*, tells of his resistance to having God interfere in his life. As each of us must, Lewis had to reach a point where he ceased to resist, consciously taking off his armor and allowing the Divine Interferer into his life, before he could become a Christian.

Christian commitment insists that we make way in our lives for the Great Interferer. Commitment in marriage insists that we allow another to share the charmed circle of our most intimate personal lives. And so, because commitment challenges at the very point of selfishness, at the very center of our willfulness and willingness, it is most costly.

Unfortunately, many people have failed to really understand the cost of commitment—especially in faith. Too many preachers, in too many churches, tell their congregations that they are forgiven—that the benefits of reconciliation and atonement are theirs—without making it adequately clear that a personal response to the Gospel is essential and that personal acceptance of what Christ offers must be on His terms: unconditional surrender.

But another whole group of preachers overlooks the cost

and undersells the values. "Come to Jesus," they say, "and you will have more money, better sex, more wins in the bowling league—more of whatever your heart desires." The cost of commitment is greater, and the value of commitment is other than what is currently being offered. Not the "cheap and unworthy prizes that worldly men set their hearts upon," but immeasurably greater benefits, are made ours. For "the whole purpose of God in redemption is to make us holy and to restore us to the image of God."[14]

But this is only at the cost of total, unreserved commitment. In the words of Thomas a Kempis, "We give the all for the all."

PART II

Making Meaningful Commitment

Commitment does not just happen. It is something we consciously do. In this section, we look at several phases in making, developing, and keeping commitment. We find that we must "grow up," in order to make mature commitment, and then we must go on growing within a commitment, if we are to make it last and bloom.

6

Commitment as Conscious Choice

Writing in *The Washington Post,* Henry Fairlie tells of a
farewell conversation with the president of his college at
Oxford. "What do you think Oxford has taught you?" the
scholar asked Fairlie.

"It has taught me to see all sides of a question," Fairlie
told him.

The professor responded tartly: "I hope that it has also
taught you to choose one."

That is what commitment is all about. The currently accepted caricature of commitment is that of a haughty
grande dame, looking sternly through her lorgnette, saying, "My mind's made up, don't confuse me with facts." In
a culture in which the greatest virtue is open-mindedness,
the corresponding vice is, of course, "closed-mindedness."
And this has become confused with commitment. Yet, ac-
tually, far from being closed, committed thinking is the
product of, and productive of, intellectual vigor. Very
often, the lack of commitment indicates the wishy-washi-
ness of intellectual laziness. It is the uncommitted person
who lacks the rigor and discipline to really examine, really
decide, really make up his mind.

Without commitment, one can acquire only knowledge. It is only through commitment that one can apply that knowledge to life and gain Solomon's desire, an understanding heart (*see* 1 Kings 3:9). Far from being a retreat from reason, commitment is the most rational thing a person can do. Recognizing the brevity of life, it makes the best of sense to survey the options and then make choices; to choose and exercise a set of beliefs that will pattern and give meaning to life; to choose a person with whom a lasting, deepening, and truly intimate relationship can be established; to answer to a vocation with dedication.

A view of man that perceives him merely as a biological entity, or even as a biological entity with reason, is short of a complete understanding of the distinctiveness of man. And when the biological/rational model is as pervasive a presupposition to cultural thought as it is at this time, there is a corresponding paralysis of the ability to make commitment.

In *Gulliver's Travels,* Swift satirizes the man who fails to acknowledge his spiritual nature in the harsh chapters describing Gulliver's visit to the Houhynhnms. As Gulliver kisses the horse's hoof, fully accepting the rule of reason without counterbalancing it with spirituality, he becomes a slave. He loses his humanity and becomes nothing more than the animal that "horse sense" tells him that he is.

When man perceives his personality and destiny as functions of uncontrollable variables of heredity and environment, he sees no reason why he should be expected to exercise sufficient self-control to enter into commitment. Intimacy and responsibility are no longer meaningful ideas.

The corrective can be found in the scriptural view of man. The opening chapters of Genesis show us a created man: a biological entity, but from the outset, unique. Man is a "living soul," with a spiritual nature to complement his physical being. He has will, together with freedom of choice. And accompanying that, he has responsibility for his choices. Putting these components together picks man up out of the dust and sets him upright in his unique place. Only in a view of man that is complete enough to recognize his complex nature as a biological, rational, and spiritual entity can the true concept of commitment move forward—for commitment requires action that is both rational and spiritual, and commitment issues in physical action. Commitment is an act of the will, based on both reason and faith. As such, it is the act that makes us most fully human, most fully adult.

Reaching the point of commitment is, in itself, a maturing process. In each area of commitment, as in life as a whole, one can see a progression—through childhood to adolescence, and finally to maturity, as commitment is entered into and made irrevocable. As we look at the actual process of making commitment, we can distinguish these phases, or periods. For some commitments, we pass through these phases coincidently with our physical childhood, puberty, and maturity. For others, we may enter into the childhood of commitment at another stage of our physical lives. Thus, a person might have matured through childhood and adolescence into a marriage commitment, without having given any thought to a faith commitment to God. At some later date, when this matter becomes important to that individual, he will have to go through the process of maturing to commitment in that area of his life, as well. The "childhood" and "adolescent" phases may be much shorter, but they will doubtless exist in some form, in the experience of making a commitment.

Childhood: Precommitment Phase

The period of life prior to affirming commitment is childhood, no matter how long it lasts or when it occurs in life.

This does not mean that the child is incapable of commitment. Many children have begun a lifelong commitment to God in preschool years.[15] And I know of at least one stable and enduring marriage built on a friendship begun when the couple were toddlers. But the combined action of reason, faith, and will, which is the essence of commitment, is a step beyond the spontaneous, "I love God," or, "I like you," of early childhood.

In commitments that are made entirely within the years of adult life, this period of "childhood" is the period when consciousness of the area of choice is first awakened. An established businessman with a stable marriage might suddenly awaken to the whole dimension of the spiritual. In that area, at the time of new awareness, he is a child.

But if we must become "as a little child" to enter into a new domain, we dare not stay as little children. A tragedy of our day is prolonged juvenilization. One senses everywhere among adults "an overwhelming desire to abdicate adulthood and return (however guiltily) to the undemanding world of childhood where no choices need to be made or justified, no responsibilities assumed or discharged, no commitment expected other than to the immediate gratification of the self."[16]

If we are to know true adulthood in the mature understanding and living out of commitment, we must reach that point to which the Apostle Paul points: ". . . when I became a man, I put away childish things" (1 Corinthians 13:11). And the way to that point is through the "adolescence of commitment"—the period of intelligent review of options.

Adolescence: Review of Options

Moving from consciousness of a choice to be made to conscious choice making is the next step in commitment. And this is an intensely rational phase. The more carefully alternatives are evaluated and the more clearly one can focus on goals, the greater the chance that a commitment can be made that can weather the tests of life.

One of the discoveries in this rational phase is that we can't have it all. One choice precludes another. The choice to marry precludes the choice to stay single. The choice to enter training for a vocation precludes the choice to "hang loose" and tour around. The choice to bear children precludes the choice to give oneself fully to one's career.

Thinking through what a choice includes and precludes is an important part of rational commitment. Paul invites us to present ourselves to God as a living sacrifice, which, he points out, is our reasonable service (see Romans 12:1).

It makes sense. The more all of our choices and commitments make sense in frank, open consideration, the more solid they will be. Of course there are few choices which do not include an element of risk. And probably there are no commitments which will not sometimes be haunted by the ghosts of "what I might have done." But entering commitment rationally, with sound reasons thoroughly thought out, will help to give our commitments staying power.

By intelligent choice, the passion and excitement of youth can be directed into a thoughtful and permanent marriage. That passion is the small tinder with which the hearth fire is kindled. There is a sudden blaze, the joyous, crackling excitement of young love. Then, the great logs in the fireplace—loyalty and compassion and sacrifice—are set alight, to continue their long, slow burn for the rest of life.

Because reasoning is such an important aspect of making a commitment, we have to come to terms with the blurring effect desire has on reason. Desire is most often translated *love*. Under the heat of desire, reason ripples and warps. Elisabeth Elliot, in her helpful little book, *A Slow and Certain Light*, writes:

> Our human desire is never more powerfully felt than when we are in love. The experience overwhelmed me, and I did not see how it would be possible at all to know God's will in such a tempest. John Greenleaf Whittier's hymn helped me greatly then:
> "... Speak through the earthquake, wind, and fire, O still, small Voice of calm!"

Hardheaded and unromantic as it may sound, if it doesn't make sense, it can't make happiness. If a person cannot find objective reasons why the other person will make a good mate, all the subjective emotions will not be enough to keep a marriage together.

In the commitment of faith, too, there is place for rational consideration. A person may enter into faith intuitively, but sooner or later he must dig some footings, if the structure of his faith is to stand. For children who enter the faith in childhood acceptance, this may come as a period of examination of the rational basis of the faith. The personal discovery of the whole field of apologetics is an important growth phase: finding out *why* it is reasonable to believe. For those who come into the faith from unbelief, there is often a period of rationally weighing the evidence.[17]

Of course, reasoning is not the only road to commitment. Some people, like my friend Jane, have quite irrational entries. "My roommate talked me into going to the meeting. I wasn't a bit interested, but I went to make her happy. The chairs were comfortable and the auditorium was hot and the message was long. So I dozed. Suddenly I heard the speaker shout, 'All of you out there who are sinners, stand up.' Startled and only half-awake, I stood up. He told us to come forward, and forward I went." That night, Jane received Jesus Christ as Lord of her life. A changed life witnessed to a true act of commitment. It was not a very reflective entry into the Kingdom, but an entry, nonetheless.

But the fact that some enter into faith by such experiences does not lessen the importance of a rational basis for faith. There are reasons for believing. Jesus Christ entered time and space and became a person in human history. And He confronts us with claims that have to be reckoned with. Just as a marriage that is begun in a flurry of infatuation may mature into a lifelong, meaningful commitment on the basis of a later understanding and acceptance of each other, so conversion experiences that are basically emotional will need the maturing process of thoughtful consideration, of time spent in the study of the Scriptures, to become lifelong and life changing.

In order to make commitment in a meaningful way, then, we must first become as little children, conscious of the area in which a choice must be made. Then we must review options and exercise choice. But commitment is more than merely "making up my mind." It has to issue in action, and that requires an act of will, a calculated taking of risks.

7

The Risk of Commitment

The young man sat, limp and disconsolate, in the big chair in the corner, his long legs stretched out. He had wool socks on, but his problem was cold feet. With romantic ideals and illusions shimmering around his head, he had asked a fine young woman to be his wife. She had agreed. But now he was confused. There had been an angry argument, followed by a sulky day. Could this really be the woman of his dreams?

We sipped at mugs of steaming coffee and talked things over with him. Had he thought he was going to marry perfection? Was what he had discovered about temperament more important than what he already knew about personality and character? Was their mutual desire to build a home worth the risk of facing, realistically, that there are no perfect people—only ordinary people who learn to accept each other?

At last, he put his shoes on again. He had affirmed his decision to marry. Life was not going to be "dreams come true," except as realities were accepted. He would take the risk. Like all who learn how to make lasting and meaningful commitments, he had to learn that it is only in taking the risk that commitment can be made.

Adult Commitment: Taking the Chance

Commitment must issue in action. Until something is done, commitment is not complete. Faith becomes saving only with confession and obedience; love becomes marriage only with the exchange of vows and life lived together.

Moving life in the direction of the choice is the essence of commitment. The archetype is faithful Abraham: "By faith Abraham obeyed . . . sojourned . . . offered" (*see* Hebrews 11:8, 9, 17). It is on the basis of faith that choice becomes commitment; by faith, decision is translated into action (see figure 2).

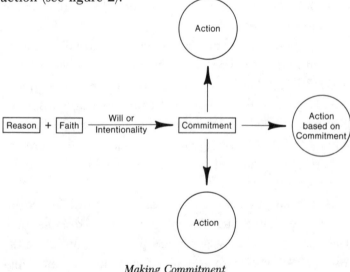

Making Commitment
(Figure 2)

Faith has become a fuzzy concept. It is commonly confused with a warm and possibly worshipful feeling. But biblical faith is not a feeling. It is an activity. It is a confidence that allows one to take the risk of commitment: not an unfounded confidence, it should be pointed out. For while faith is, at times, "a leap in the dark"—it is not a leap into darkness without light, nor is it essentially irrational. It is based on a reasonable assurance that what we hope for may be.

The moment of the actual exercise of faith, or making of a commitment, is a moment of intense conflict. The person who is considering the step is most aware of an overwhelming sense of risk. "If I do this, what about the other alternative that I am hereby rejecting?"

I remember the day that a minister friend of ours signed his membership card for the political party that my husband was representing in an election. He had long supported another party, but in support of Cam's candidacy, he made the new commitment. Under the blue fluorescence of our kitchen light, he looked at his new membership card before slipping it into his wallet. "Dear Lord," he whispered, ashen faced. "I hope that this is not the end of all that I hold dear."

That is what the moment of commitment always feels like: the end of all that I hold dear, and the hope that it is not. The moment of commitment is always a moment when the risks appear huge. This awareness of risk may last for many months, as described by Saint Augustine in his *Confessions*. The sense of risk begins to subside at the moment at which commitment is made—never before.

Thus, making a commitment requires a decisive moment which, though illumined by hope, is fraught with risk and a sense of intense peril.

I remember experiencing this exhilarating—and panicky—sense of risk as I stood at a mail-order counter and ordered my first dishwasher. With tiny children, I had been struggling to find time to write, endlessly frustrated by the never-enough hours of the day. Those were the days when the dishwater cooled and jelled while I kissed away hurts, rushed toddlers to the bathroom, and endlessly changed and washed and folded diapers. Often, I would get back to breakfast dishes about the time lunch had to be prepared. Time to write? I didn't even have time to get the dishes done.

And then, late in a dismally wet harvest season, one of my friends phoned. "Guess what I got for my birthday," she exulted. I couldn't, so she told me. "A dishwasher! It's the greatest thing that ever happened to me," she told me. "It saves me an hour a day."

Suddenly I wanted a dishwasher very much—not as a thing in itself, mind you. It was that hour a day I coveted. If I could just make an extra hour in each day, I could write. I mentioned the dishwasher = time equation to Cam, who was still struggling to finish harvest. He was not very interested. With exquisite sense of timing, I pressed the discussion until I got a final answer. Cam thought the dishwasher was a wonderful idea. He would be delighted to buy me one—when he could afford it. Meanwhile, I could bear in mind that our mothers had managed just fine without dishwashers. . . .

It was clearly a subject to be dropped. I dropped it reluctantly. Having prayed fervently, even feverishly, that Cam would see how much I needed that hour a day, I finally wrote in my journal, "Dear Lord, I give You my hands anew—to whiten and wrinkle in dishpan suds." It was very maudlin, and not even slightly accurate. My hands never stayed long enough in the dishpan to whiten or wrinkle, and our water was so hard, there were never any suds. But finally, I felt peace. I had laid my desire down.

Only then did an amazing thought strike me. I could provide the dishwasher for myself. The plan was simple, but breathtaking. I would order the dishwasher. With the hour a day it freed for me, I would commit myself to write for publication. With the proceeds, I would pay for the dishwasher.

For a submissive, house-bound housewife, the risk was enormous. But that churning, spluttering machine did free me for an hour a day. And I did write. I had to! The moment I placed my order, commitment was made. Aware of risk, I took a step of faith and committed myself to writing. It was a clear and unequivocal starting point, full of risk and hope.

I remember, too, the night we decided to trust God and plunge back into farming. After ten years of farming, we had had to liquidate our assets, to settle with our creditors. Low market prices for cattle and an early August frost had literally wiped us off the board. We didn't know what to do next. Should we move to the city, take teaching jobs, and start a new life? Apply to a mission board? We could have traveled pretty light, just then!

That winter, through a series of miracles, we found our-selves able to reassemble a farm. Now, the harrowing question was whether we should purchase machinery and farm again, or rent out the land and let someone else take the risk.

Finally, Cam found a clear sense of direction. It settled in on him through the reading of Scripture and through prayer. He wakened me one night, to tell me his decision. He would farm again. I will never forget the mental re-lease that came with that decision. It was like coming out of limbo, into life. Suddenly, life had purpose. We had things to do, decisions to make. The risk was there, but so was the hope. We had made commitment.

Career and business commitments—and even marriage commitments—are minor, compared with the one com-mitment that lasts forever: the commitment of the life to God through faith in Jesus Christ. For all who have made this kind of commitment, the wilderness of wondering is familiar. A thousand questions bother us. What will Christ ask of me? How will He change me? Will I ever have fun again? Will my friends turn against me? And the big, cen-tral question: Can I believe that Jesus is the Son of God? We face, individually, the dilemma of Peter, as he pon-dered Jesus' question: ". . . whom say ye that I am? . . ." (Mark 8:29).

> To fail to worship God: Impiety.
> To kneel to mortal man: Idolatry.
> With all to lose, I slowly bend my knee.
> Oh, Son of God and Man, I kneel to Thee.

I remember how it was for a university colleague of ours. Cam had pulled the car in to the curb. Frost hung in the air, haloing the streetlight, that bitter January night. The three of us continued our conversation. It had been going on for a couple of hours that night, but intermittently it stretched back over several months. Questions had been asked, and answers attempted. And now there were silent spaces between our words. The lanky student had run out of questions, it seemed.

"Anything else you need to work through?" we asked.

He shook his head. "No. That seems to be about it."

"Remember," Cam said, "you can't understand it all until you make a commitment. It's like walking down to the barn, you know, carrying a lantern." Our friend shared Cam's rural background. He understood the illustration immediately. "You have enough light for only a step at a time. The circle of light moves as you do."

We sat silently, sensing his personal struggle. Then we asked, "Did you want to make your commitment to God now?"

He was silent for a few more seconds. "Might as well," he said at last. The potential benefits had outweighed the thousand risks.

And in that cold, black and silver northern night, we sat in our car with bowed heads to witness his commitment of faith.

He prayed, unprompted, "Dear God, I believe that Jesus Christ is Your Son and that He died for my sins and rose again. Here's my life; take it now and forever."

Many years have passed. Our friend is today a university

professor, quietly living by the inner light that came into his life that winter night, glad he took the risk of faith.

Every commitment is a sort of gamble. But for the person experiencing the acute sense of risk that comes at the moment of making a decisive commitment, there is a dual risk: Not only the risk of exercising faith and making a commitment, but the equally acute risk of *not* exercising faith and making a commitment. It is what Sheldon Vanauken describes so well as the "gap behind"[18]—the sense that one cannot draw back from the risk that is to be taken, except at even greater risk. The human adult must constantly choose to take risks, for there is no risk-free living that is worthwhile.

Commitment is not irrational. It would be foolish to trust a foothold you have not properly tested, or to marry a person you have not adequately assessed, or to trust a message you have not investigated. But commitment requires more than reason. It requires the act of faith: that shifting of weight, that trusting of oneself. And then, as commitment is made—and the rope does hold on its mountain hook—the sense of risk fades and hope grows.

8

Sealing Commitment
in Sacred Ceremony

The sealing of commitment by sacred ceremony has long been part of the cultural and religious life of every people. Once a commitment has been considered and entered into, in the mature way that we have been discussing, there is every reason for celebration, every reason for calling together members of the family, or of the church, to witness with solemn joy the entering into of that commitment.

Today, however, the increasingly careless attitude toward the permanence of commitment works against these sacred sealing ceremonies in two ways. Serious young people, angered by the hypocrisy of those who use sacraments without seriousness, decide that they can exchange vows to each other in privacy, with at least as much meaning. Not-so-serious adults don't want sacramental trappings to what is essentially a private and negotiable contract. And in between lie the great mass of those who do not think very deeply at all, who use sacred ceremony as tradition, without concern for its meaning, or who flippantly dispense with it.

In an age of change, is there still any meaning in the ancient, sacred sealing of commitments? Are ceremonies such as confirmation or baptism, to seal the commitment to faith; marriage, to seal the commitment to another; and ordination, to seal the commitment to vocation, mere relics of the past?

Obviously, the point could be argued both ways. In the last year of my teens, I was married in a traditional church cermony. But in my twenties, I found it hard to find much meaning in the ceremony. I saw so much cynical abuse of sacred ceremony that I wondered what its use could be.

Marriage counselor Russel Dicks satirizes contemporary marriage in an unforgettable vignette:

> Assuming that sexual expression is irresistible, like a flood, many couples inevitably find themselves standing before a minister to be married. Minister: "Do you take this woman with all her immaturity, self-centeredness, nagging, tears, and tension to be your wife, forever?" The dumb ox, temporarily hypnotized by the prospect of being able to sleep with her every night, mumbles, "I do." Then the preacher asks the starry-eyed bride who is all of eighteen, "Do you take this man, with all his lust, moods, indifference, immaturity, and lack of discipline to be your husband, forever?" She thinks that "forever" means all of next week, because she has never experienced one month of tediousness, responsibility, or denial of her wishes, so she chirps, "I do," in the thought that now she has become a woman. Then the patient minister parrots. "By the authority committed unto me as a minister of Christ, I pronounce you man and wife. . . . " As he does, he prays a silent prayer for forgiveness, for he knows he lies. They are not now husband and wife and he knows that few of them ever will be. They are now le-

gally permitted to breed, fuss, bully, spend each other's money, and be held responsible for each other's bills. It is now legal for them to destroy each other, so long as they don't do it with a gun or a club. And the minister goes home wondering if there isn't a more honest way to earn a living.[19]

In my thirties, I have grown to understand more of the value of the "community of faith" in supporting commitment—the importance of the church as a bearer of witness to one's significant, irrevocable commitments. But probably it was an event, rather than an argument, that really changed my mind.

That event was the wedding of my friends Isabelle Jones and Ray Johnson. That wedding, so carefully planned that every moment of it reflected glory to their Lord and Saviour, Jesus Christ, convinced me that Christian marriage could be a high holy day, with a truly sealing significance upon a maturely made commitment. For my friends, I wrote a brief sketchbook of memories from which, with their permission, I share:

The Presence of God was everywhere in the wedding. His Presence had been invited—or, perhaps—announced, by the cream invitation cards mailed to all the earthly guests, on which the down-descending Dove hovered over the flames of two earthen lamps.

In this symbol of the invited and acknowledged presence of God's Spirit was the first notice of the Presence of God Himself, which would hallow and sanctify every moment of Isabelle's and Ray's wedding. Aware that the flame of their love issued only from earthen lamps, the bride and groom had asked that the Spirit of God would fan that flame with His eternal whisper of Love.

It was that Presence which made this wedding so special. His Presence was not only felt in the strictly "spiritual" things: in the minister's exhortation, in the vows, or in the words of parental counsel. It was everywhere, in all things. Indeed, it was His Presence which took the tasteful blend of sacred and secular, of sacrament and celebration, and hallowed all. Jesus Christ was Lord of this wedding day. It was a festival of praise to Him, a glad Christian celebration of man and woman, of husband and wife, of love and of marriage, of God.

There was so much beauty today. The bride was incandescent. Her maturity was emphasized by the severe simplicity of hairdo and veil that swept away all distraction and made one look with wonder at the face of the bride, who had "Today put on perfection, and a woman's name." Details of dress and adornment could be noticed only later. As we saw her step into the aisle and walk toward her young husband and her new role, there was only her face to consider: a beautiful, mature face, lit with tenderness and sincerity. A bride. A beauty. A woman.

The groom was eclipsed, until he stood to reply to the toast to the bride. And then it became clear why he had won her—a young man who spoke with candor and conviction, who was not afraid to risk tears to mention his beloved mother who had recently died, or to speak of his anticipation in sharing with Isabelle their mutual faith in Jesus Christ as Saviour and Lord.

Coming together to celebrate on the wide, green lawn walled by evergreens were people of many backgrounds: village and city folk, friends and family, they visited and shared in the joy of the day. At supper time, the recep-

tion was both feast and festival: good food in rural pleni-
tude, served with neighborly grace and hospitality, com-
plemented by a festival of music of the highest caliber.
From the guest artists' bossa nova interpretations to the
quartet of young male voices affirming "Great Is Thy
Faithfulness," all issued as praise to the Creator—
". . . who giveth us richly all things to enjoy" (1 Timothy
6:17).

And then, it was over. It was hard to let them go, calling our good-byes and best wishes. They left ready for
high flight up above the clouds and tumultuous emotions
of courtship, into the calmer, brighter skies of marriage.

Since the time of Isabelle and Ray's marriage, I have
been to many weddings. Some few have touched on the
glory of true Christian celebration of a binding and permanent commitment. Many have missed out on both the
Christian and celebratory aspects. In some weddings
I have attended, there has been precious little for anyone
to celebrate. And when I hear young couples exchang-
ing limp vows that are to be binding only "as long as we
both shall love," I find I hardly have the heart to lift a
toast.

Of course the ceremony is only as significant as the
commitment which it seals. But despite many disappointments and some reservations, I have come to believe that
commitment that is not sealed by some public act of celebration is unsupported and weakened by its privacy. The
sealing of commitment before God and "so great a cloud of
witnesses" (of which the gathered believers are only a
fractional representation), is a solemnizing and affirming
act, underlining the significance of the commitment that is
made.

For a marriage to have its fullest expression of commitment, there must be a sealing commitment at three levels: before man, before God, and before each other. A marriage which consists of only a private, unsealed commitment lacks the sacred sanction of being sealed before God and the legal sanction of being properly executed before man. Christians who are serious about sealing their commitment as a lifelong and non-negotiable part of the structure of their lives will seek to enhance the meaning of each of these three levels of sealing. Thus they strengthen their private commitment with the witness and encouragement of friends, family, and fellow believers, and with the fullest consent to legal requirements. They will flout contemporary convention and reserve sexual consummation until the marriage is sealed before God and man.

While marriage is the sacred ceremony of which we are all most aware, there are, of course, other important sealing ceremonies within the Christian tradition. The one that is invoked to seal the commitment to vocation is ordination. It is interesting that, despite the breakthrough "discovery" of the Reformation that anyone's work, offered up to God, constitutes vocation, the Church has never adjusted its sacred ceremonies to reflect this fact. We still ordain ministers, lay hands on missionaries in commissioning services, and ignore the equally sacramental nature of others' daily work. We need to work toward what Elton Trueblood calls the abolition of the laity. As young people come to understand the true meaning of vocation and answer in discipleship, the Church should respond, to seal such commitments by sacred ceremony.

Elizabeth O'Connor, in *Call to Commitment*, includes a service written for the Church of the Saviour in Washington, D.C., for this purpose. I am not suggesting that the Church commission people at every change of job. But when a person finds God's call to lifework, then that call and commissioning might well be confirmed by Christian witness and public confession. Thus, the theological notion of the priesthood of all believers could be translated into terms which all of us could understand, emotionally as well as intellectually: "As a teacher, as a farmer, as a secretary, as a plumber—I am called to minister. And this fact has been recognized by my brothers and sisters in Christ, who have confirmed my calling and commissioned me to serve in it."

The prototype of ordination can be found in Jesus' commissioning of His disciples and again in Acts: ". . . Separate me Barnabas and Saul for the work whereunto I have called them" (Acts 13:2). The calling of the individuals comes first; the ordination and commissioning by the Church follows and imparts strength to the calling. Every believer who has reflectively answered God's call to the ministry of a particular task in life could well be given the support and encouragement of ordination.

The commitment to faith in Jesus Christ as Saviour and Lord has always been attended by sacred ceremony in Church history. At first, baptism on confession of faith was the rite. Later, as children were born to believers, infant baptism became more and more widely practiced, as a sort of "advance entry" into the Kingdom, with confirmation becoming the key confessional ceremony. Today, infant baptism, followed by confirmation—or believer's baptism on confession of faith—are the chief rites of inclusion in our churches.[20]

I recall the summer Sunday when our oldest son was baptized by immersion. The sacred celebration took place at a nearby lake, where the church family gathered in a sheltered cove. Out on the lake, motorboats dashed back and forth, with skiers fluttering behind. But in the little bay, where the sandy shore curved around the water, we were in a sanctuary. The mood of the occasion was that of solemn joy—an emotion rarely experienced in our world. As the candidates for baptism stepped out, one after another, into the water, and publicly confessed their faith in Jesus Christ and their lifelong commitment to live in "newness of life," the fellowship of the church family flowed around that circle of faith, engulfing each confessing believer in the love and acceptance of those with "like precious faith."

Whether confirmation or believer's baptism forms the rite of inclusion, the church should wholeheartedly enter into sacred celebration of commitment. Commitment rites should be *voluntary*, depending upon the personal desire of the participant to make public confession of faith. The ceremony should be *based upon a personal confession of faith*, and not serve as a ritualized substitute for such confession. It should be carried out *before the body of believers* with whom the confessor is fellowshipping. And, within whatever formal structures are chosen, there should be place for both spontaneous personal confession of faith and traditional, formal elements.

With such sacred celebration as we have discussed in this chapter, the Church should continue to confirm and infuse with the truth of the Gospel the individual commitments of its members. "God is here, let's celebrate." For commitments are strengthened by a sealing act. Sealing a commitment in sacred celebration impresses significance, encourages endurance and brings God's grace to bear on the fulfillment of that commitment.

9

Growing Within Commitment

Since I have the original purple thumb, it's great that Cam loves to grow things. He asks me to leave his plants alone, since they seem to wither as I pass. So I keep my distance from them. Yet, as I watch Cam husband his plants, I get a new understanding of the way in which commitment allows for personal growth.

In the first place, you can't grow all the plants you want to grow in one pot, or even in one planter. Selection must be made. And once you have decided what plant to grow, any other plant, no matter how interesting or virile, becomes a weed. It just has to go. This matter of selection is, of course, a matter of simple, basic commitment. One particular pot is committed to growing begonias—not begonias and something else—just begonias.

"Narrow-minded!" someone cries.

"How dreadfully stagnant."

"Locked in . . . and too fearful to widen!"[21] But as the begonias begin to bloom, the wisdom of selection begins to be more obvious. And thus it is in life, as well. The committed life may not have the luxuriant growth of a weed patch, but the bloom makes selectivity worthwhile.

Commitment does not mean stagnation and narrowness. It means that a principle of selection has been put into effect. It means that growth is not random, but planned and purposeful. It means the possibility of bloom in the life, which is impossible without the careful tending, selection, and devotion of good husbandry.

Recognizing that we do not have time in life to follow every inclination, pursue every kind of knowledge, or develop every kind of skill, we must choose those to which we will give our energy. Without commitment, the diffuse personal growth advocated by so many writers today can only produce confusion: a dozen little, stunted plants in the plot of one's life. Commitment says, simply: "I've only got this one space in which to grow my life. So I can't grow everything. I will choose what is most important. Other kinds of growth will be weeded out; not because they do not have life, but because they do not contribute to the development of the growth that has been chosen." Then we begin to grow within commitment.

Growth in Knowledge and Understanding

It is only upon making commitment that we can really understand the complexities of any area of life. Trying to fully understand marriage without being married is impossible. Similarly, the person who knows all about the Christian faith, without having committed himself to Christ, knows nothing, in comparison to the simplest believer who has made the commitment of faith and finds the living

Christ within him. However, having made that initial step of commitment, every believer has the potential for limitless personal growth, as he comes to a clearer knowledge of his faith and an increased understanding of how to live it out.

With every commitment comes the need for growth in related abilities and skills. The development of a truly satisfying sexual partnership requires skills learned within the underlying commitment. The mechanical approach to sexual activity, which is so widely promulgated today, is a far cry from the development of expertise within a permanent, lifelong relationship, where the sexual activity is not an end in itself, but part of the total commitment. And so it is in all commitments. There are skills and abilities, related to any commitments, that can only be developed to their highest point within those commitments. I may have an interest in law. I could read widely in the area of my interest. But my knowledge of legal matters and my ability and skill in using that knowledge would always remain rudimentary, compared to that of a practicing lawyer. The difference? I have not made a commitment to that vocation, while he has.

Growth in Capacity to Care

Commitment not only promotes and creates conditions for growth in knowledge and understanding. It is also a prerequisite for *growth in the capacity to care* for others besides oneself. It is only when commitment has been made and affirmed that we have the capacity to leave our engrossment with self and reach out to others, not for self-gratification, but in genuine self-giving and caring.

My sister-in-law, Marg Jones, a nursing instructor at the University of Alberta School of Nursing, addressed the graduation exercises of a recent class. Her comments on that occasion, to a group of professional "carers," clearly defines this often-overlooked link between commitment and caring.

In sharing with you today, one theme seems to be more important to me than all the rest. It is a theme that you reminded me of consistently those months that we spent together.

It was just about three-and-one-half months into your program, late afternoon, and time to go home. Bundled up in my winter togs, laden down with books, and tired, I noticed a little note that had been slid under my office door. Picking it up, I read a note from one of you. I'm not sure which one of you, because you signed no name. In this little note was an expression of thanks for my care of you as a person. This stopped me short, I put down my books, sat down, and re-evaluated my anxieties with my new role. Yes, I had to work hard at developing teaching skills, but most important to you, I surmised, was that I continue to *develop my ability to care*. . . .

The profession of nursing, in which you now officially belong, demands that a nurse care. Any definition of nursing has an explicit statement or an implicit assumption that a nurse should care. The public expects that a nurse will care and is bitterly disappointed if they encounter one who doesn't. . . .

I believe that the ability to care is directly related to our success at finding personal purpose and meaning in life. Questions such as: "Who am I? Why am I here? What happens to me when I die?" have been asked by individuals since time immemorial. If an individual finds personal answers to these questions, he will possess the inner security and strength that is necessary to enable him to risk reaching out to share another's burden—to care!

You are developing toward becoming caring people. Each of you have a personal and unique path toward becoming mature, caring nurses. I have watched with the greatest of interest, as you left my classes and moved through all the other phases of your training. You have developed a growing confidence in your ability to nurse. Some of you have found particular areas of nursing for which you seem perfectly suited. Each of you is more capable of giving care than you were two-and-one-half years ago. Whether you have consciously identified it or not, each of you is searching for personal purpose and meaning in life. I challenge you to make this search a conscious pursuit and a priority in your life. . . .

For each of you wonderful new nurses, my deepest wish is that you will search and find out who you are, why you are here, and where you are going. For your ability to give real care to patients, to people, will be directly related to your success at finding personal meaning and purpose in your life.

Not only for professional, paid "carers," but for all of us, in all of our interactions, deep personal commitment is foundational to the development of the ability to care. I am stirred each time I approach a large, city hospital and see the intensity with which people walk toward the doors, drawn to the bedsides of those they love. They carry gifts: flowers, books, candies. And their faces mirror their concern. As I watch, I wonder. Who will visit the sick, when commitment is finally eroded? Who will care if another human lives or dies? Caring, one of the beautiful blooms of commitment, is the result of the patient growth and development of commitment. It can come no other way.

Growth in Trust

Another of the results of growing and developing commitment is *growth in trust.* When I read in Proverbs 31:11 of the woman in whom "The heart of her husband doth safely trust . . ." I sense the deep, quiet rest within a relationship of total commitment, the serenity of safely trusting each other. This doesn't come about in a few years. It grows with the loyalty and fidelity expressed and shown. As commitment is not only made, but cultivated and tended, trust buds and blooms into something beautiful. Our ability to safely trust in each other is endangered by the push and pull of our worlds. Working women share the same temptation to infidelity that was once the province only of husbands. But temptation lasts only until a firm "no" is said.

Having made and meant commitment, speaking warmly and positively about one's mate to business associates and other contacts can serve to nip advances before they are made. I remember a conversation with a business executive on one flight. It wasn't long before he asked, "What do you have planned when you arrive?" I told him I had a speaking itinerary. "Maybe we could get together," he said. "Or is your husband jealous?"

I just laughed. "No. He's not jealous. He trusts me completely."

It is only within commitment—made, meant, affirmed, and growing—that trust can develop. What a beautiful thing it is to live with; what a deep, personal freedom.

Only the person who has made firm commitments can be truly an open person. Every new idea does not threaten his life structure; every new friendship does not threaten his marriage. Within the framework of irrevocable commitment, a woman can meet men as brothers, a man can meet and treat women as sisters. A faith commitment, too, allows a person to be open to others. One who has made a personal commitment does not need to be defensive, closed, and hostile. He does not need to have all the theological answers, in order to maintain his commitments. If he has truly found a central point to which all other aspects of life can relate, he can meet, with caring and love, even those who differ angrily from him.

I know a young woman who had her life turned around by the unthreatened, open responses of a fellow student. Surprised to find him a Christian, she threw angry arguments at him: "How can you say there's a God of love, when there is all this suffering?" she said. "I'm astonished at your simplemindedness."

The young man didn't have pat answers. "I don't know all the answers," he said. "All I know is that Jesus is for me." The young woman was so shaken that she investigated the Gospel for herself. Today, she is a minister of that good news.

True commitment allows for the growth of all that is good and positive in our lives: growth in knowledge, understanding and skill; growth in the capacity to care, to trust, to be open. Commitment is, in fact, a prerequisite to growth as a person.

10

Commitment That Endures

We grew used, one winter, to seeing a neat, little half-ton being driven carefully down our country roads. The old man at the wheel was making his daily trip to the hospital, to visit his wife. Paralyzed by a stroke, she could no longer speak. Many days she showed no sign of recognition, but he went to sit beside her, to reach out and hold her hand: to say, after fifty years of marriage, "I love you." His vigil never faltered; his daily trip was made through blizzards and thaws, throughout that long winter until her death.

The old man, sitting in silence beside his wife, had once been the young farmer, driving team and wagon to pay his respects to the neighbor lass. Then he had had everything to gain by making the effort. Now, commitment had matured through the years, to create this greater kind of caring: love that could give without expectation of receiving anything in return.

Such love is hard to cultivate in today's climate of self-gratification.

A young woman I know was recently diagnosed as having a rapidly progressing deteriorative disease. Her doctor called her husband in for consultation. "You might as well

leave her now," he told the husband. "She'll never be anything but a burden to you." And so a couple, struggling
with the strain of adjusting to a long-term health problem,
also struggled with the question: "Why stay together?"
And, as long as the question was phrased, "What is there in
this for me?" the husband's answer would have to be the
same as the doctor's.

That couple, instead of forsaking each other, forsook the
doctor. They found another, who could give psychological
support to their commitment to each other.

In *The Luck of Ginger Coffey,* novelist Brian Moore describes Coffey's breakthrough into understanding the
meaning of committed, married love:

> Love isn't an act, it's a whole life. It's staying with her
> now because she needs you. It's knowing you and she will
> still care about each other when sex and day dreams,
> fights and futures—when all that's on the shelf and done
> with. Love—well I'll tell you what love is: It's you at sev-
> enty-five and her at seventy-one, each of you listening for
> the other's step in the next room, each afraid that a sud-
> den silence, a sudden cry, could mean a lifetime's talk is
> over.[22]

It is this kind of insight that is completely lacking in the
"how to cope" pop-psychology writing of today. Adult
commitments, we are told, cannot be expected to last
longer than seven years. The old "seven-year itch" is perhaps more than mere fable. But adult life, chopped up into
a series of seven-year segments, with the emotional wast-
age of change in major areas repeated again and again

throughout life, is a tragically discontinuous kind of existence.

Built into the concept of commitment is the concept of endurance. To hedonistic thought, the idea of "enduring" anything is repugnant. The very connotation of endurance is that of putting up with inconvenience, difficulty, even hazard. How can we reteach it as a virtue, to a world increasingly addicted to instant gratification? The prevailing mood is that when something ceases to satisfy me, my commitment to it is thereby rendered null and void. In other words, commitment need last only as long as there is something in it for me.

I have yet to find a contemporary book that teaches the concept of endurance as faithfully as John Bunyan did in *Pilgrim's Progress.* The Christian life is not a matter of saddling up faith and riding into a sunset of promise. And those who do not realize that bound into a confession of faith is a commitment to endure, cannot hope to withstand the assaults of faith and commitment that will lie ahead. Jesus said trenchantly, "But he that shall endure unto the end, the same shall be saved" (Matthew 24:13).

Endurance is often not accompanied by emotional concomitants such as joy or peace. It is often a holding pattern, where with Hudson Taylor we say, "I will trust Him where I cannot trace Him," or, with Job, we cry out the ultimate words of faith: "Though he slay me, yet will I trust in him . . ." (Job 13:15).

In his study *Love and Will,* Rollo May stresses the importance of intentionality in love. Intentionality, he points out, is far more than mere intention. It is the application of the will to the making of a decision. It is precisely in this area of intentionality that many modern commitments are deficient. Barnabas exhorted the new believers in Antioch that "... with purpose of heart they would *cleave* unto the Lord" (Acts 11:23, *italics mine*). When Adam was given Eve, the pattern was established that "Therefore shall a man leave his father and his mother, and shall *cleave* unto his wife ..." (Genesis 2:24, *italics mine*). That's intentionality. Cleaving is clinging in the firmest possible sense: Not merely intending to honor a commitment, but backing that intention with the firm set of the will.

In contemporary literature, I find the most moving story of enduring commitment to be that of the prisoner Nerzhyn and his wife, Nadya, in Solzhenitsyn's *The First Circle*. Cultural pressures are entirely against their continuing to honor their marriage commitments. For Nadya, marriage to a political prisoner is a dark shadow over her studies and career. For Nerzhyn, there is no future hope of consummation. He and his wife grow older, without opportunity for so much as a kiss. Both Nadya, in her university dormitory, and Nerzhyn, in his work prison, have opportunities to cast away their commitment to each other. No one in their society would find such infidelity inexcusable. But, tempted to a relationship with another man, Nadya affirms her commitment to Nerzhyn. As she turns away from the other love offered, "She stood like someone crucified on the black cross of the window. There had been one tiny little spot of warmth in her life, and it was gone. And in only a minute or two she had resigned herself to that loss. She was her husband's wife again."

On the other side of the prison wall, Nerzhyn works out his commitment. Offered the opportunity of a sexual liaison with a woman government official—a liaison which could have brought amelioration to his condition, perhaps even termination to his imprisonment—Nerzyhn rejects physical consummation outside of his marriage commitment. In the very tense and difficult scene in which Nerzyhn explains his lack of response to the woman who had offered herself, he says, "I love only her. . . . She has killed her youth for my sake . . . I must go back to her alone." As they die to other possible relationships, Nerzyhn and Nadya experience the resurrection of a purified commitment. And as they do so, they rise above our expectations and become saints.

We could well have forgiven them infidelity. But they are ennobled by their fidelity, and the literature of the human race is ennobled by them. In a world of tawdry selfishness, love that holds no hope of personal reward but nonetheless continues to burn with a blue flame must be one of the most God-like of human virtues.

Where will we find understandings and concepts upon which we can build the virtue of endurance? First we will need to recover a sense of *adult responsibility and accountability*. The basic dignity of humanity lies in responsibility for our actions and decisions. Implicit in the idea of responsibility is that of accountability. We are creatures accountable to our Creator; we are the redeemed, accountable to our Redeemer. The sense that we must give account for ". . . the things done in . . . [the] body . . . whether it be good or bad" (2 Corinthians 5:10) must permeate our thinking, if we are to hold to a position in which commitments, once made, are honored at great cost.

We need to seek life's meaning in *some other goal than happiness.* Happiness in the human experience is never achieved when it is made an end in itself. Like the pot of gold at the end of the rainbow, it continues to beckon. Who ever finds the rainbow's end? But when commitment and loyalty are given their proper places in life, happiness is the by-product discovered with surprise some quiet morning.

Commitment, like the amaryllis, does not produce continuous bloom. You know how the amaryllis grows. In the early spring, it shows life, sending up dark, smooth leaves. Then comes the great central stalk and the exhilarating beauty of the great trumpet-shaped blooms. But after the amaryllis has bloomed, it goes into a period of dormancy, when the best thing that can be done with it is to set it in a cool, dark place and wait for further signs of life. But no house gardener would throw away the amaryllis because it has stopped blooming. Enduring means simply this: Don't throw away the amaryllis. There may be a period of dormancy.

In religious commitment, this may be a time of doubt, a time of dryness. In a marriage, it may be a period of groping for new channels of communication, of adjusting to differential aging, of accepting new interests on the part of one's spouse. In vocation, this may be a period of feeling "flat," of having achieved one's goals and not yet found new goals to set. But in each case, the least mature approach is to throw out the commitment because it is not in bloom. The fact is that commitment, like the amaryllis, if allowed to endure, will bloom again—and again.

"Behold, we count them happy which endure . . ." (James 5:11). There is, in enduring commitment, a quality of peace that is perhaps the highest joy known in the human experience. It is the peace, or tranquillity, of having some things settled. It is the serenity of knowing loyal love to be of higher value than lust, and compassion to be a greater emotion than passion. It is, in the religious experience, the ability to believe when there is no sign, the growth of faith in the darkness and silence that brings it to bloom in the light.

11

Commitment as Covenant: A Caveat

I have expressed the ideal of thoughtful, continuing, enduring commitment in several key areas of life. Yet, as I write these chapters, I am keenly aware that there are those who have made commitment ill-advisedly. They have committed themselves to people, to projects, to groups—and they have hit a dead end. There is no possibility for heroism, or even for personal growth, in their commitments. In the "urge to merge," they have made commitments: to a marriage, to a cult group, to a job situation. And now, everything has turned into a nightmare.

The bleak question is asked again and again: Now what?

Because we are fallible persons, because we continuously miss the mark (which is the literal meaning of the Greek work translated *sin*), there must be some way of canceling out commitments that destroy. A mistake in job choice, friendship, or religious affiliation may cause disruptive change. The mistake should be acknowledged as soon as it is clearly recognized. Withdrawal from any of these commitments may well be painful but necessary. Many a businessman has faced the mopping-up operation after a business commitment has gone sour: an employee has betrayed trust; a partnership has failed; a venture has proven to be disastrous. To endure, in the face of very obvious evidence that a mistake has been made, is scarcely heroic. It is, more often, pigheaded.

In good faith, a person may have joined a religious group. Now, however, he feels a strange unease. He has made commitment. But he senses that he has been betrayed. If, upon a careful reading of the Word of God with the prayer, "Shew me thy ways, O Lord; teach me thy paths. Lead me in thy truth, and teach me . . ." (Psalms 25:4, 5), that person senses that he has been led into error, then there is only one thing to do. No matter how difficult, the cords that bind must be cut.

I remember talking with a friend who had floundered into a heretical cult. "Jack," I said, "if I thought someone had sold you a life-insurance policy that could not pay the promised benefits, I would have to tell you about it. And I feel that you are being offered unfounded hope through a works-based religion. The real Gospel is that God's grace, extended to us in Jesus Christ, is our only hope of eternal life. And I have to tell you that I think you have a worthless insurance policy." I couldn't encourage him to "hang in."

God invites us to enter into covenant relationship with Him. The bold business bargain struck by Jacob: ". . . If God will be with me, and will keep me in this way that I go, and will give me bread to eat and clothing to wear, so that I come again to my father's house in peace, then the Lord shall be my God" (Genesis 28:20, 21 RSV) is a very personal example. God calls out, through His prophet,

Malachi: "... put me to the test ..." (Malachi 3:10 RSV).
We have a God who can stand the test of proof, who is as
good as His covenant implies. In instituting the Lord's
Supper, Jesus explained that He was ushering in a New
Covenant, sealed with his own blood. And the terms of
that, too, appear almost as business deal. "If we confess our
sins, [*then*] he ... will forgive our sins ..." (1 John 1:9 RSV).
Or again, "... if you confess with your lips that Jesus is
Lord and believe in your heart that God raised him from
the dead, [*then*] you will be saved" (Romans 10:9 RSV). It is
because God keeps His promises that we can enter into a
relationship in trust. What God has said, He will do—
without variation or favoritism. Any religion that offers
less—or more—cannot bring us into the covenant of grace.

When we turn to the much more complex and delicate
matter of marriage, I have to add a caveat, too. Many
Christian spokesmen claim marriage to be an unconditional commitment. Elton Trueblood writes:

> Everyone recognizes the degree to which marriage is a
> bold venture, undertaken without benefit of escape
> clauses. The essence of all religious marriage vows is their
> unconditional quality. A man takes a woman, not, as in a
> contract, under certain specified conditions, but "for
> better, for worse; for richer, for poorer; in sickness and in
> health." Always, the commitment is unconditional and
> for life. The fact that some persons fail in this regard does
> not change the meaning of the glorious undertaking.[23]

As much as I like the ring of those words, I have to dis-
agree. I believe in thoughtful commitment, growing com-

mitment, enduring commitment. But the idea of totally unconditional marriage terrifies me. That would mean that my husband could beat me, be unfaithful to me, be non-supportive of me, and still be entitled to be my husband. I agree that marriage is not a contract, but something far more binding than a contract. I believe that, in its basic nature, marriage is a *covenantal relationship* between two persons. And being covenantal, it is sacredly solemn and binding.

Underlying marriage vows is the basic, universal covenant of marriage, reaching as far back as the presentation of Eve to Adam, by which two became one. Anything less than "leaving" and "cleaving" does not constitute full, covenantal marriage.

Young people who marry with a shrug, "If it doesn't work out, we can always call it quits," or who premise their marriage on some private covenant, "If either of us finds somebody more attractive, we are free to pursue another relationship," are only kidding themselves that they are truly married. They are merely living in legally licensed adultery.

Short of exclusive and total commitment, marriage becomes little more than a game: going steady, raised one power. And—as those of us who have gone steady know—the whole point of that game is how to handle the breakup. The inevitability of breakup is acknowledged. The smart "steady" knows how to bail out just before the other one does—giving, rather than receiving, the hurt of rejection. Sadly, this pattern, built on mistrust, is being practiced in many marriages today.

Marriage is not only covenantal in its underlying commitment, but also covenantal throughout. It is a lifelong series of "if . . . then" clauses, implicit or explicit, by which a man and a woman work out the bargain and compromise of living together. Probably the most basic underlying commitment is, "If you will be kind to me, then I will be kind to you." Whether stated as baldly as that or not, it is a theme that runs through every good marriage.

There is an economic covenant implicit, too, for marriage creates a new economic unit. In the older-style, traditional marriage, the understood financial covenant was, "If you will make a home for me—make my meals and mend my socks—then I will go out and work and support you and the children you bear." This has been replaced in many modern marriages by an equally reciprocal covenant: "If you will help me reach my goals within the framework of this marriage, then I will help you reach your goals within the framework of this marriage. If you will share fully of yourself and your resources with me, then I will share fully of myself and my resources with you."

In addition, many couples work out covenants in various phases of their lives. Today couples who are trying to build a lasting marriage, in which two aspiring adults can find fulfillment, are working out shorter-term covenants such as these:

"If you will help me finish my education, then I will pledge myself to help you finish yours."

"If you will bear and take primary responsibility for the nurture of children, then I will care for you financially and help you return to your career."

Marriage is reciprocal, as is covenant: It is giving and receiving, loving and being loved, supporting and being supported. The more clearly a couple understands the covenantal basis of their marriage, the better they can live up to their covenants.

Like everything else in our twisted and sin-scarred world, the sacred covenants of marriage are often twisted into threats, unholy and selfish in their nature. The very nature of threat denies the underlying marriage covenant of cleaving, and a couple that hurls "if . . . then" threats at each other is pulling down the framework of their marriage.

Jesus' teachings on marriage, which so clearly state the divine ideal of permanent, enduring relationships, still point out that adultery is a just ground for ending a marriage. Adultery is the turning away of love from the one to whom it has been promised, toward another object. "Adultery," says James Olthuis, "covers all the ways in which infidelity in marriage can take place. Due to the structure of marriage, infidelity of various kinds usually leads to infidelity on the physical level."[24]

Paul, too, points out the ideal of permanent, total commitment, when dealing with the specific problem of what to do when one partner in a marriage relationship becomes a Christian. He upholds the ideal that marriage is to be lasting; a marriage is not to be disrupted because one member becomes a Christian. Yet in his discussion of marriage in 1 Corinthians 7, there are two memorable "but" phrases. One is for the believing wife: "But and if she depart, let her remain unmarried or else be reconciled to her husband . . ." (v. 11). The ideal: Stay together. The exception: If the relationship is totally unworkable, separate. (This option, it must be noted does not open out on divorce and the freedom to remarry. It opens out into celibacy and hope for reconciliation.)

The second "but" clause also concerns a marriage in which one partner has become a Christian: "But if the unbelieving partner desires to separate, let it be so; in such a case the brother or sister is not bound . . ." (1 Corinthians 7:15 RSV). If the unbelieving partner has initiated the separation, it appears that the believing spouse is free to remarry. Death, of course, is the other biblical cause of marriage dissolution, leaving the living spouse free to remarry.

It would appear to me that each of the "exception clauses" in the teachings of Paul and of Jesus is for *breach of covenant,* which is, basically, infidelity. Yet, it must be noted that in the Old Testament, God raises the idea of covenant to its highest level. Even when Israel is faithless, God remains faithful to His covenant. Through the graphic and painful story of Hosea's wooing of his adulterous wife and, by grace, gathering her back into his home, God shows how far His love will reach beyond the terms of His covenantal agreement.

The Old Testament prophets revealed the amazing truth that the covenant can continue to exist because of the faithfulness of only one party. And this holds out the same hope for marriage that Paul holds out: ". . . the unbelieving husband is sanctified by the wife, and the unbelieving wife is sanctified by the husband . . ." (1 Corinthians 7:14). Over and beyond the terms and conditions of covenant, the "... love of God [which] is shed abroad in our hearts by the Holy Ghost ..." (Romans 5:5) can enable us to choose to endure in a covenant relationship in which we are not obliged to remain.

There are, of course, some situations in which separation seems to be the only reasonable course. Even Paul allows for this. Such a decision cannot be based on simple disagreement, or even on what is so often referred to as a "communications breakdown." Disagreements can be resolved by compromise and communications rebuilt with counseling, if there is the will on the part of both partners to make the commitment endure.

But in cases where one partner is suffering physical abuse, or where a partner with an alcohol or drug dependency refuses treatment or rehabilitation, or where criminal, incestuous, or other immoral behavior of one partner threatens the well-being of wife or children, a separation may be necessary. Sometimes, the trauma of separation may be needed, to force a drug- or alcohol-dependent mate to seek help. Sometimes, the separation forces a reconsideration of the basic covenant of marriage, and the marriage can be rebuilt with new and deeper understandings of the commitment involved.

Because the essence of marriage is reciprocity, the concept of covenant is uniquely fitted to the marriage relationship. Covenant allows the necessary "escape clause" to keep marriage human. Yet it continuously illumines the relationship with sacred solemnity and seriousness of purpose.

PART III

Areas of Commitment

We have considered in some depth the meaning and making of commitment, drawing most of our illustrations from the two basic commitments of life: faith and marriage. Now we turn to consider some other areas that are enriched by commitment: commitment to family, to a believing community, to vocation, to principle.

12

Commitment to Family

> Looking at human behavior with all that we know—and can infer about the life of our human species from the earliest times, we have to realize that the family as an association between a man and a woman and the children she bears, has been universal. . . . The evidence indicates that the couple, together with their children, are everywhere at the core of human societies.
>
> —Margaret Mead[25]

It took Margaret Mead quite a while to get this insight together, but there it is. The family is universal, central. And commitment to it is essential to the survival of a society or of a person. Gradually, the truth is dawning on us that the uncommitted person is the big loser; that life without continuing, binding, identity-affirming commitments can hardly be called life at all.

Serious young adults today are making tough decisions, recognizing that sacrifice is entailed in making the choice between being family-first people and work-first people. As Ellen Goodman writes:

A friend refused to move up a rung on the professional ladder because it would have meant uprooting his family and transferring his wife out of a career of her own. Another couple consciously put their careers on the back burner in order to spend time with the family. . . . These were not bitter choices, but tough ones.[26]

Because we have already dealt in considerable depth with the commitment of marriage, in this chapter we will take a look at some of the other bonds of family, and what they mean.

Commitment to Children

I remember a conversation with a young couple a few years back. We were discussing the role of women in government.

"What do you think of a woman in politics?" Tom asked.

I shrugged. "I guess I'd have to ask, 'Which woman?' What are her abilities? priorities? I'd ask the same questions about a woman in politics as I would about a man in politics."

Tom frowned. "Well, I'm opposed to women in politics, because it interferes with good mothering," he said.

Having just come through a political campaign with my husband, I replied, rather tartly, "And what about the things that interfere with good fathering?"

More and more, young parents are coming to terms with the commitment involved in having children. More and

more, a committed corps is making the sacrifices necessary
to ensure their children of the stability and security, not
only of good mothering, but also of good fathering. The
"invisible father," whose main contribution to family life
was a paycheck, is becoming a less dominant model to
many young parents whom I know. Fathers and mothers
are finding ways of sharing the nurture of small children,
so that they can both enjoy, and both endure, the tasks of
parenting. This pattern is meaning that both parents set
career goals in the number-two position during the early
years of parenting and that they consciously consider the
welfare of the family, as a whole, ahead of the personal interests of either partner in the marriage.

Because bearing children is a choice today—and, in the
face of antifamily propaganda, a choice that needs to be
consciously worked out and even defended—young people
who choose to parent are perhaps making that choice
more carefully, more awarely than ever before. The commitment to bear children should certainly entail the commitment to love and nurture those children, to give them
the very best hope of developing to their whole potential.
And that requires an end to "me first" thinking, if marriage
hasn't already dealt it a deathblow. It requires cooperat-
ing with God's great plan that out of love should come life
and that family love should nourish and sustain that life.

Not that children need to have the highest priority in
our lives. They need to know that we have lives and interests and ministries that sometimes include and sometimes
do not include them. We dare not merge our identities

with our children. We must encourage them to be persons separate from us, as we continue to be identifiable persons apart from "mummy" and "daddy."

Neither, of course, should our children be the unseen guests in our homes. They need to have a place in our love and in our time, which encourages them to see themselves as people of worth. They need to know that we enjoy spending time with them. (And that, by the way, is possible only if they are pleasant and polite—in other words, well trained and consistently disciplined. Parents who do not train their children never enjoy them, either.)

We must be aware of our children's needs to develop self-esteem and, as they mature, to recognize their own gifts and calling under God. For these discoveries, the family provides a framework of love, stability, selective opportunity, and discipline.

These things we owe to the human beings whom we bring into the world. If, in the process of helping our husbands or wives know and use their gifts, or in the process of discovering and using our own gifts, we should fail to help our children develop fully, we will have failed sadly. For it is the contribution to the next generation, which we make in and through our children, that will be most lasting. Ministering to, and ultimately through, our children will be the greatest multiplier of our own ministries.

Yet we will do our children the greatest of favors if we help them see themselves not as the centers of any universe—including our own—but as important components within significant and active adult lives: as fellow planets in a solar system centered in the Sun of Righteousness. This will be learned not through sporadic outbursts of affection or attention, but in day-to-day attention: in awakening creative and curious minds determining standards, in developing wholesome habits, in every way preparing our children so that they might be "meet for the Master's use."

Most of all, our children need to be treated as people, individuals of worth and distinctness, individuals who are deeply loved and who have a place in God's plan for loving this sad world.

Parenting has three distinct phases: "hanging in" with preschool children, to give them the best possible basis for development; "hanging on" with older children, training them to become independent decision makers by gradually broadening the areas in which they can make decisions, while ruling out areas in which decisions could scar or mar them for life; and finally, "letting go." Every phase is fraught with danger and laden with opportunity.

It is in that release of our children into life that the parent-child commitment seems to be most perilously jeopardized. If we let them go, will we lose them? And then, as with all the other paradoxes of life, we learn that it is only in letting go that we find them.

Letting go, of course, begins at the moment of birth. The cutting of the umbilical cord symbolizes the parting to come. Then comes weaning. Next is school, as we begin to share our children with a wider world. When our children reach legal maturity or leave home for college or a job, we must loosen our hold still further.

When our children choose to marry, we must let go, no

matter what we think of their choice. If we are disappointed, we may lovingly express our opinions before the matter is a *fait accompli.* After that, we must keep quiet and pray. Our loving acceptance will build bridges, if needed, for them to return to the love of God and to us.

Our ability to part with our children reflects our confidence in God. If we trust our children or trust our good upbringing methods, we'll be disappointed. If we claim the promises of God concerning our children, we will have His grace to let them go.

Yet there is a sense in which we never let our children go. Like Job, we pray for them daily, continuing the prayer ministry we had to them before their birth. If our grown children have no warm love for or service to the Lord Jesus Christ, then how earnestly we will pray. But that is all. We will not pester. They know what we desire. If we have been faithful in our teaching, they know the way of salvation and restoration. We must respect their freedom, trusting a Father who loves them more than we do to bring them back to Himself.

Recently I discussed some of these principles with a group of women. One mother who had said good-bye to all her children shared a promise she had claimed for erring children: "If his children forsake my law, and walk not in my judgments; If they break my statutes, and keep not my commandments; Then will I visit their transgression with the rod, and their iniquity with stripes. Nevertheless my lovingkindness will I not utterly take from him, nor suffer my faithfulness to fail" (Psalms 89:30–33).

As we claim such a promise, we will take our cue for action from the father of the prodigal son. In the story of the prodigal son, the father let go when the son demanded his adult privileges. The father accepted his son's adulthood and right to make decisions, even though he must have doubted his son's management ability. And later, that father did not interfere with the natural consequences of the son's actions. He could have bailed the son out of the pigpen and brought him home, but he was too wise for that. He realized that the son would have to make his own decision to return. When the son did come back, he found the father's loving, forgiving welcome.

Only as we let our children go can they become the men and women God intends them to be. Only so, can we fulfill our commitment to them. More selfishly, it is only in letting them go that we can receive them back as friends.

On a Mother's Day recently we took my parents for a picnic. As I visited with my mother, she commented, "You know, I had a card from all you children this year!" We laughed. Usually, at least one of the four forgets.

"I think I know why," I said. "Parents just get more and more special. I know that, as I experience my children, I am becoming more aware of all that you have done for me. You have never meant more to me than you do right now."

That's how it is. Letting our children go, in accordance with God's Word, means getting our children back. It is only as we release them from answerability to us that they are able to come to us as confidantes. And, although very different from the parent-child relationship, the commitment of adult children to their parents is a bond even more wonderful, because it is a chosen relationship.

Commitment to Parents

And that, of course, brings us to commitment to parents. It is our first intuitive commitment—that natural, reflexive response to the trustworthy nourishers of our childhood. But it is a commitment that must be superseded, if we are to create a new family unit, by our commitment to a mate. A man must leave his father and mother as number-one commitment, in order to properly cleave unto his wife, and vice versa. But while the commitment to parents may be superseded by commitment to mate, it is never an unimportant one. The commandment, "Honor thy father and thy mother," with its accompanying promise, is not written for children. It is written for adults.

However long they live, our parents deserve our respect and love because, simply, they are our parents. Because they have given us life, there is a debt of honor to be paid, and we are enjoined, "Render therefore to all their dues . . . honour to whom honour [is due]" (Romans 13:7).

Sometimes, this isn't easy. It is particularly hard if parents refuse to take their new place in the commitment hierarchy, below one's commitment to God and commitment to mate and children. Parents who continue to attempt to control, who interfere in the lives of married children, may be hard to honor. Yet the command stands. We honor them then, not in obedience, but in deference; not in allowing their control, but in extending every courtesy. Honoring our parents includes attending to their needs as they age. If those needs are financial, they become our responsibility. If they are emotional—and perhaps this is more often the case, encompassing the need for companionship, for love, for being accepted—we must do what we can to meet those needs. For like all other interpersonal relationships, the commitment between parent and child is reciprocal: The love and nourishment received in childhood should be reciprocated in love and personal care given to aging parents.

Commitment to Siblings

Family commitments allow not only for the commitment to mate, to children, to parents, but also for the lifelong bond between siblings. Writer Robert Thomas Allen describes a scene in which he talks with his older brother:

> We stood ... two gray-haired gents, while he gave some directions, looking at me just the way he did when he was eleven and I was eight. . . . It was a good feeling knowing that there was still someone who cared if I got lost. But there was a lot more to it than that. Even better was the feeling, as we stood there on the sidewalk ... that we were surrounded by a kind of spiritual crystal lattice formed of concern, comfortable habit, responsibility, experience, and memories. The invisible lines of force that make up that special structure—the family.[27]

Of course there are disappointments, frictions, unhonored covenants and dishonored vows within family. Modern writers have made us fully aware of this. Honesty requires our own admission of it. But the beauty of the pattern is still discernible. Commitment to family continues to be the most meaningful and satisfying of human relationships. The Jewish tradition, in which Christianity is rooted, is one in which the family unit is the very basis of society. The Garden of Eden focuses attention on the marriage commitment as primary, ahead of all other relationships, except with God. Genesis is, above all else, a book of families: troubled families, torn families, but families which, through all the honestly recorded friction and heartache, became the base of a nation, a chosen people.

In the New Testament, the concept of family continues to enshrine the ideals of the Garden of Eden, redeemed now by the death of Christ, so that marriage becomes a mirror in which the union of Christ and His Church is to be seen. And now, the concept of family widens from political and national significance, to include the whole family in heaven and earth. The Christian view sees the family as central, with its extension of love being not so much the clan or the nation, but the Church fellowship which—like the family itself—reaches across generations, to give continuity to the whole of human existence and meaningful continuity in each individual life.

13

Commitment to Christian Community

The young woman visiting with me was aglow with a new faith experience. "Tell me," I said, as we trailed our fingers in the cool, amber river that borders our pasture, "are you involved in a good church fellowship?"

"Well," she said, "yes and no."

I waited for her to explain.

"I've been going to a church the last few months where they have a really great emphasis on the gifts of the Spirit. But for the next few months, I'm going to go to another one. I understand that it really has a special emphasis on prophecy."

I tried to explain that she was missing the whole point of commitment to a believing community. "It's not the sermon topics, but the communion with God and with caring Christian brothers and sisters, that counts. And to experience that, you can't flit from congregation to congregation. You have to find a local fellowship in which the teaching is true to the Word of God, and then cast in your lot. Be there every Sunday, and you'll learn what it is to be part of a local body."

I don't really think she heard me. A few months later, I

learned that she was ill and unemployed. Who cared? Her casual contacts in several churches? A minister who had preached to her for half-a-dozen sermons? I don't know who reached out to her, besides her own family. But I know that if she had committed herself to a fellowship really worthy of the name of *church*, there would have been those who would have shared her pain.

Too many people choose their church service as they would choose a movie. They go where the action is: a big-name speaker, a controversial topic, a way-out performing group. But in doing so, they miss out on the deep sharing and caring that is the result of true commitment to a church fellowship.

Commitment to Jesus Christ presupposes commitment to His Church. John Stott says bluntly:

> The Christian life is not just our own private affair. If we have been born again into God's family, not only has He become our Father but every other Christian believer in the world, whatever his nation or denomination, has become our brother or sister in Christ. . . . But it is no good supposing that membership of the universal Church of Christ is enough; we must belong to some local branch of it. . . . Every Christian's place is in a local church sharing in its worship, its fellowship and its witness.[28]

In the "hang loose" mood of our day, the importance of firm commitment to a local church is often overlooked. The result is that Christian commitment becomes highly individualized, and thus impoverished. Commitment to *the* Church is best affirmed in commitment to *a* church.

Many young believers find themselves frustrated with the church as they find it, and rather than attempting to make a contribution within the structure as it exists, they opt out of the church family. The church, of course, may take one of many forms: the house group, the assembly, the huge congregation. But commitment must be made to fellowship regularly with other believers, if a person is to truly disciple himself to Jesus Christ. The writer of the book of Hebrews advises sternly that we are not to be ". . . forsaking the assembling of ourselves together, as the manner of some is . . ." (Hebrews 10:25).

There are, of course, no perfect churches. There is no one fellowship that has a corner on the only New Testament model. Indeed, it seems as though perhaps the best understanding of denominational choices was voiced by a friend who said, "You choose a church according to your spiritual temperature. Some people like to run hot, some like to run cool." Accepting this diversity within the Body is a mark of maturity. But simply drifting from one fellowship to another, in search of perfection or a fresh charge for spiritual batteries, can never create the experience of "Body life" that is meant to be a very vital part of the Christian experience.

Commitment to the Church carries with it many of the benefits of commitment to family. In the larger family of the Church, in friendships and caring that cross generational, racial, spatial, and even time boundaries, a sense of the continuity of life is gained. The little particle of life of each individual becomes a part of a great whole: not lost, but given a setting, a meaning, and an extension. Within the Church, ". . . ye are all the children of God by faith in Christ Jesus. . . . There is neither Jew nor Greek, there is neither bond nor free, there is neither male nor female: for ye are all one in Christ Jesus" (Galatians 3:26, 28).

It is by the *communication* of the Gospel—the good news that ". . . God so loved the world, that he gave his only begotten Son . . ." (John 3:16)—that we are invited into *communion*. It is no accident that the Table of the Lord, by whatever name and through whatever form of service it is approached, is central to the worship of believers. Paul, in reviewing the Lord's Supper for the Corinthian believers, reminds, "For as often as ye eat this bread, and drink this cup, ye do shew the Lord's death till he come" (1 Corinthians 11:26). In the communion fellowship, we look back to Christ's death with gratitude and forward to His coming with anticipation, and we are strengthened to go on sharing with our brothers and sisters in the task of bearing witness "till He come." Whether as Eucharist at an ornate altar, or as the loaf broken at a simple table, this remembrance meal binds all who have named the name of Jesus Christ into one vast fellowship. It is a fellowship that stretches around the world. It stretches back through all the ages of Church history, to that moment in the Upper Room, when our Lord Himself broke bread and offered the cup "in remembrance of Me." It stretches out ahead of us, until the consummation of the age in the coming of Jesus Christ as King of kings and Lord of lords. And it wonderfully presages yet another supper, at which our Lord will preside; a supper at which all Christians of all centuries, all the great "Company of the Committed" will celebrate their unity with one another and be finally fully united with their Lord (*see* Revelation 19:7–9).

If the human family lends meaning and continuity to life, how much more so "the whole family in heaven and earth" (*see* Ephesians 3:15). In the Church Universal, one finds oneself as part of Christ's continuing presence here on this earth. In the local fellowship, one has opportunity to interpret this in practical relationships of caring and sharing.

Not only should the Church contribute to continuity and extension of the individual life; it also should help to provide purpose and meaning. For the Church does not exist just for the comfort of Christians. It is through the Church and by the Church that God continues to reveal His truth from generation to generation. And every member of the Church, every committed Christian, is part of that vital transmission of truth. We have a job to do, and we find it expressed within the context of the Church. The Church fellowship should be concerned about identifying and giving opportunity for the use of the gifts of the Holy Spirit among its members. And here again, a sense of personal mission, fused with the great, overall mandate of the Church to "Go . . . teach . . . baptize . . . preach . . ." (*see* Matthew 28:19 and Mark 16:15), lends meaning and order to life.

Commitment to the community of believers that is the Church is not a way of ducking out of commitment to the "global village" of mankind. It is a way of finding and harnessing my abilities and gifts to God's redemptive purposes for His fallen creation. It is a way of finding out what I can do to witness for Jesus Christ, as part of a whole fellowship similarly committed. It is a way of being strengthened to serve God by serving mankind.

It was a Christian poet who crystallized a concept that has captured the imagination of so many modern writers:

> No man is an Iland, intire of it self; every man is a peece of the Continent, a part of the maine; if a Clod bee washed away by the Sea, Europe is the lesse. . . . Any mans death diminishes me, because I am involved in Mankinde. And therefore never send to know for whom the bell tolls. It tolls for thee.[29]

It is through a deep and enduring commitment to a fellowship of believers—a community of the faithful—that we learn how to feel our kinship to others, and ultimately to all humans. Peter Jenkins, who found a personal relationship with Jesus Christ during his walk across America, had expected that those who would try to help him along the way would be "young, hip, long-haired, college-type people." But this was not the case. "You know, I'm kind of thick headed. But it began to get to me that every person that reached out to me was a Christian. . . . The young, hip, intellectual college generation of our time . . . were very rarely the ones who tried to reach out and help me."[30]

Through the caring of committed Christians, Jenkins found himself surrounded by the love and care of God and made part of the very community he had attempted to reject.

Learning through the Sunday-by-Sunday worship and week-by-week sharing of life with other believers, we fi-

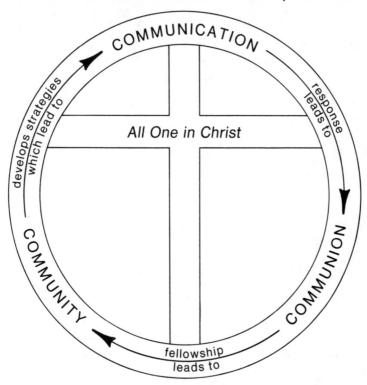

The Unity of the Witness, Worship & Work of the Church
(Figure 3)

nally come to an understanding of what it means to be
"members one of another." And in awareness of both our
unique personal identities and our corporate identification
with all believers, we are enabled to become serving, caring people in our communities.

14

Commitment to Vocation

The year was 1784. A boy of fourteen was deposited at a sketchy fort on the shores of Hudson Bay, apprenticed for a seven-year stint of work in the Canadian wilderness with the Hudson's Bay Company. Disconsolately, the teenager wrote in his journal: "When the ship sailed and from the top of the rocks I lost sight of her, the distance became immeasurable and I bid a long and sad farewell to my . . . country, an exile forever."[31]

As the son of a poor widow, the boy had had no choice about his assignment. Circumstances beyond his control dictated his daily work. How easy it would have been for him to have merely done the chores expected of a fur-trading clerk, nursing resentment at his fate. Instead, David Thompson found within his circumstances a vocation. He made it his life's work to bring the immense and uncharted wilderness of the West into the realm of human knowledge.

With determination matched by brilliance, Thompson turned the dreary days of travel in an empty West into a long song of praise to his Creator, bringing the best of his abilities as a navigator, astronomer, and cartographer together with his writing ability, to give us both a geographical and historical account of the West as he found it.

Fame did not come to him. His maps were pirated and reprinted above the imprint of other names. But as one reads his narratives and recognizes the clear, blue flame of devotion with which he conducted his daily work, one cannot doubt that at his homegoing, David Thompson heard the words of his Master: ". . . Well done, thou good and faithful servant . . ." (Matthew 25:21). Tardily enough, historians have discovered how great a contribution Thompson made to North America. He stands as a giant: a Christian who lived out his commitment to God through his commitment to a vocation.

Commitment to vocation is a strong, cohesive force in life—and one of which, in our free, individualistic society, we have nearly lost sight. Housekeeping, building, cobbling—all constitute calls from God, invitations to share in His work of tending and renewing His creation.

Today, the sense of "call" has been all but lost. Industrialization, materialism, and secularism all have taken their toll. Industrialization has made man feel that, when he works, he is basically a machine. The assembly line has produced generations of workers who are separated from the finished product—hence, separated from any sense of satisfaction or meaning in their work. Materialism has meant that the only reason to work is to make money, in order to buy consumer items. The idea of work as service to God and to mankind, with the wage as a by-product necessary for sustenance of life, is so lost as to seem laughable. For most workers, the only meaningful aspect of work is the weekly paycheck. Secularism means that most people live separate from any sense of God in their lives. Even Christians find themselves living in a compartmentalized world, with Sunday being dedicated to spiritual things and Monday through Saturday to the material.

Because we have lost the sense of being called of God to fulfill a particular place in His world, we tend to think of our work as of our own choosing. Thus, we feel committed to no one but ourselves in the fulfilling of our tasks. We have "jobs" rather than "vocations." We do not sense an answerability to God for the way in which we do our work.

The alienation of man from his work is the subject of much discussion. I do not think it is a phenomenon peculiar to our society. One cannot think that the medieval serf experienced any great satisfaction in his work. Indeed, it was a part of the curse that resulted from the Fall that work should become servitude. But work itself was not the curse. Adam and Eve were given tasks long before the Fall. The effect of the curse was to rob work of its joy. For the Christian workman, however, work has been honored by Jesus' participation in it, redeemed by His death, and given meaning by His lordship in our lives. The New Testament affirms the goodness of work: "Whatever you do, do your work heartily, as for the Lord rather than for men; knowing that from the Lord you will receive the reward of the inheritance. It is the Lord Christ whom you serve" (Colossians 3:23, 24 NAS).

Our day-to-day work should be seen as our calling. Our exercise of the calling then becomes a part of our spiritual exercise—a truth seen and lived out by Brother Lawrence, the monk who strove to discover "how to become wholly God's."

"I will have no will but that of God," Brother Lawrence wrote, "which I endeavor to accomplish in all things, and to which I am so resigned that I would not take up a straw from the ground against His order, or from any other motive than purely that of love to Him."[32]

Certainly, many Christians would aspire to such a union of worship and work. But few really discover how to bring the two into meaningful focus, how to keep what Luther called the "right hand" kingdom of the Spirit and the "left hand" world of everyday living in perfect balance.

> The believer is compelled to live in both kingdoms. . . . The word of God will come to him in all his human relationships, and his work on behalf of his fellow men will be at the same time an affirmation of trust and praise toward God.
>
> In this context, any sort of serviceable status in society, through which one may serve his neighbors, deserves to be regarded as a divinely ordained calling. . . . There is no such thing as a profane or merely secular order from which God is absent, and in which God is not to be served.[33]

Obviously, if we are to consider lifework as vocation, rather than merely as a means of making a living or satisfying our urge to consume, if a sense of calling is to bring cohesion into our lives, we will have to become more serious about finding our vocation—hearing the call of God in our lives to whatever task we may undertake.

An old Jewish proverb says, "God gives you the task. He does not ask that you succeed, but He does ask that you not lay it aside." Finding the will of God for our lives is essential to making commitment to vocation.

I recall one young man telling me how he found guidance for his life. "I just think through what I would like to do, and then I figure that God wants me to do the opposite." What a negative and defeating approach to the matter of vocation! It misses out on God's wonderful awareness of the individual, attested throughout Scripture, of His knowing us before our birth and designing that our individual uniqueness will find its place in His service. The idea that "God will get you" has hindered many a young person from full surrender. I remember a liberating click in my mind when, as a teenager, I suddenly realized that God's will is not only "good and perfect" but also "acceptable" (*see* Romans 12:2). Another misunderstanding is the belief that to learn God's will you have to stifle yourself, deny that you have a will that tends in a certain direction. Elisabeth Elliot, reminds us that it is not only unnecessary, but impossible, to annihilate our own will before praying to God for His.

The struggle Jesus had in the garden of Gethsemane showed this. A conflict was taking place—not to annihilate His own will but to accept the will of the Father which was *other* than His. It did not end with Jesus saying, "My will is now thine" but with "Not my will but thine be done."[34]

God's wonderful plan for each believer's life is that he might be ". . . conformed to the image of his Son . . ." (Romans 8:29). It is not tied to geography or job description. Living in the will of God is not an exercise in tightrope walking—one step to the left or right landing you in the net. No, "For this is the will of God, even your sanctification . . ." (1 Thessalonians 4:3). There is a holy sense in which we love God and do what we want. The believer brings his life and presents it as a living sacrifice—daily. He makes himself wholly available to God. He reads the Word of God daily, so that his mind is transformed, so that he sees life as God sees it—a short, important testing ground and preparation for eternity.

And then, with an honest assessment of interests and abilities and opportunities, the believer makes a choice of vocation, through which he can live out his calling from God Himself. Whether it be pastoring a church or driving a cab, the believer will make his choice on the basis of how best he can use his abilities and interests to bring glory to his Lord and Saviour Jesus Christ. As A. W. Tozer says:

The "layman" need never think of his humbler task as being inferior to that of his minister. Let every man abide in the calling wherein he is called and his work will be as sacred as the work of the ministry. It is not what a man does that determines whether his work is sacred or secu-

lar, it is *why* he does it. The motive is everything. Let a
man sanctify the Lord God in his heart and he can there-
after do no common act. All he does is good and acceptable to God through Jesus Christ. For such a man, living
itself will be sacramental and the whole world a sanctuary. His entire life will be a priestly ministration. As he
performs his never so simple task he will hear the voice of
the seraphim saying, "Holy, Holy, Holy is the Lord of
hosts: the whole earth is full of his glory."[35]

The Christian sense of vocation lies in knowing that—
over and above circumstance, union bosses, employers,
and the drive gears of machinery or bureaucracy—we
serve the Lord Jesus Christ. In whatever ways we learn to
offer up the boredom or joy of daily work as part of the
presentation of ourselves as a living sacrifice, we contribute to making work, and therefore life, meaningful.

As the concept of vocation is once again united with our
daily work, we will be liberated from work as a curse, so
accurately described by Studs Terkel in *Working.* In a
book which "being about work is . . . about violence," Terkel mentions passingly the "happy few who find a savor in
their daily job . . . a meaning to their work which is over
and beyond the reward of the paycheck." This is surely a
beatitude that should belong to the Christian. Whatever
his particular calling, his general one is to serve the Lord
Jesus Christ. And in that glad service, the rhythms of work
and leisure unite in one hymn of praise.

A little sign that hangs inside the Home for Dying Des-
titutes, in Calcutta, expresses the commitment to vocation
lived out by Mother Teresa: LET EVERY ACTION OF MINE BE

SOMETHING BEAUTIFUL FOR THEE. It is this kind of commitment to vocation that can help bring a sense of order and cohesion to our lives as productive, working adults. Only so will our worship be united with our work and our lives made whole.

15

Commitment to Principle

Come on.... The good time is now, magnificent,
apocalyptic, on God's scale, a time of struggle between good and evil, a time for decision, in which
there is no place for the lukewarm and the coward.

Oh, how Saint Paul would have loved to live
today.

—Georges P. Vanier[36]

What the world needs now is not just love, sweet love.
Love without commitment is love without value; love
without principles lacks both direction and energy. What
the world needs now, in the most acute possible way, is
conviction: the energizing power of compelling commitment to principle.

Yet, living as we do in a Niagara of words, deluged by
information, we often find ourselves unable to form opinions, let alone realize convictions. Lacking undergirding
values and commitments, we tend to content ourselves
with knowledge, rather than pressing on for principles.
Thomas Griffith writes perceptively, in *The Atlantic:*

Active morality is a kind of side issue on today's campus,
where the main courses are brought to you untouched by

human hands, shiny, clean, and value-free. The kind of
detachment that is imperative in the sciences gives sanction in other fields to the worst of contemporary evasions:
accountants who look only at the numbers and avert
their eyes from skulduggery; lawyers indifferent to con-
duct so long as it can be profitably defended; theorists of
behavior who can no longer say that any action is worse
than another, just different. Value-free becomes value-
absent.[37]

The thinking of today is dominated by those who attempt to form opinions "free from moral prejudice," on
the basis of evidence which "strains toward scientific evidence." The educated person feels extremely hesitant
about expressing an opinion that is not based on statistics
from so-called research.

And so we are debilitated by our lack of commitment to
moral principle. We lack the kind of conviction that has
traditionally turned the turbines of social change. Whether
that is Christian conviction, such as gripped the seventh
Earl of Shaftesbury and made him devote his life to promoting legislative reform on behalf of the working man in
Great Britain in the last century; or whether it is Marxist
conviction, such as propelled Mao Tse-tung to recreate
China; if anything is to be changed, ever, it will be because
conviction compels men to act.

It is clear, however, that while commitment to principle
is as energizing as it is uncompromising and unequivocal,
it can only take society toward good goals if the principles
to which commitments are made are good ones. Where

should such principles be sought? The very ideas of right and wrong, of good and bad, of direction for improvement, demand judgment: moral judgment. Our Western roots in Judaism, as well as in Platonism, demand that we look for moral absolutes, that we trace our best instincts back to a moral law to which all earthly judgments must be submitted. Cicero argues persuasively in *De Legibus* that:

> Justice is one; it binds all human society, and is based on one Law, which is right reason applied to command and prohibition. Whoever knows not this law, whether it has been recorded in writing anywhere or not, is without justice.

C. S. Lewis picks up the theme, arguing in *Mere Christianity* that all mankind knows an underlying law by which actions can be judged as right and wrong, independent of culture or tradition:

> Human beings, all over the earth, have this curious idea that they ought to behave in a certain way, and cannot really get rid of it. . . . They do not in fact behave that way. They know the Law of Nature; they break it. These two facts are the foundation of all clear thinking about ourselves and the universe we live in.[38]

Whether we acknowledge these moral absolutes or ignore them does not in any sense change the absolutes themselves.

The only way that I see out of the modern dilemma of

widespread acquisition of knowledge and equally wide-spread lack of the values—by which this knowledge can be turned to understanding and harnessed to human need—is to recover the sense of absolutes that exist universally out-side of ourselves. Surely, the best exposition and applica-tion of these absolutes can be found in the revelation of Scripture. As we turn to Scripture, we get out of the end-less marshland of relativism and discern those absolutes to which we can make commitment and out of which can grow true conviction. Through the Word of God, we can learn to think God's thoughts.

Understanding and interpreting the Bible will call on us for the deepest of scholarship, the widest of perception, the humblest of approach. Jonathan Edwards laid down the basic rule of biblical interpretation thus:

> Spiritually to understand the Scripture, is rightly to un-derstand what *is in* the Scripture, and what *was in* it be-fore it was understood: 'tis to understand rightly, what used to be contained in the meaning of it; and not the making of a new meaning.[39]

While learning to think God's thoughts after Him may sound to some like the height of arrogance and to others like an utter impossibility, it is the challenge issued by Jesus Christ Himself. He said, "Be ye therefore perfect as your Father which is in heaven is perfect." It will demand saturation-level knowledge of the Scriptures, the devo-tional knowledge of God through prayer and meditation, and then a practical application to our society of the truths learned in study and devotion.

Principles, based on a balance of love and justice and learned through the Scriptures, can alone form a valid basis for Christian social action. Without the base of principle, like Stephen Leacock's horseman, we saddle up and ride off in all directions. But with commitment to principle, we can work toward meaningful solutions to many pressing problems. Some of these can be resolved within our own life circles: sound attitudes toward work and leisure; responsibility in the earning and use of our money; ethical principles worked out in family and other personal relationships. At this level, were all of those who claim an evangelical faith in North America to be rigorous and insistent upon applying the principles of the Bible in daily life and work, the overlapping circles of influence would dynamically change our culture.

At another level, Christians must answer the challenge of thinking God's thoughts at the governmental level. Two honest and challenging contemporary records of Christian men grappling with problems at the political level are Mark Hatfield's *Between a Rock and a Hard Place,* and Douglas Roche's *The Human Side of Politics.*

Hatfield is a Baptist and an American; Roche is a Roman Catholic and a Canadian. Each brings to his work and writing an underlying sense that, without conviction, without commitment to principle, there would be no purpose to his being involved in politics. Hatfield's theological analysis places the state and government as part of a world system opposed to spiritual values. Roche sees the Christian's work as striving to bring God's Kingdom to fruition here on earth, through human means. Nonetheless, both men are living out convictions in the political arena.

Says Hatfield:

> Political service must flow out of . . . commitment. Convictions about war and peace, about the priorities governing the expenditure of federal funds, about the patterns of economic wealth and distribution, about the stewardship of our nation's resources, about the government's responsibility toward the oppressed and dispossessed both in our land and throughout the world, about our nation's system of law and justice, and about the meaning of human liberty—these should be at the core of one's desire to seek public office.[40]

And Roche says:

> It is time for a new kind of political leadership based on a declaration of values. And that entails bringing some philosophical beliefs concerning key moral issues onto the floor of the House of Commons. . . . I am convinced that Solzhenitsyn and Heilbroner and the other prophets of our time are right. There is no hope for western leadership in an explosive world if we do not base our political judgements on moral values.[41]

Most political parties today can claim for themselves "the extreme center," which simply means pragmatism. What is popular, what will enable the party to retain power, is right in political terms. However, within this cynical tradition, we need—as never before—to hear the prophetic voice of Christian statesmanship.

In seeking to ameliorate conditions of human need through personal action or through government intervention, the evangelical Christian will continue to yearn for the return of Jesus Christ as the ultimate hope of this threatened planet. The Earl of Shaftesbury spent his total resources of money and strength in his lifelong commitment to aid the oppressed wherever he found them. Yet on his tomb was inscribed his lifelong prayer: EVEN SO, COME, LORD JESUS.

When Ernest C. Manning was about to retire from active participation in the political party that he headed for a quarter century in Alberta, a tribute was paid to him by Dr. Walter Johns, then president of the University of Alberta. Johns chose lines from Wordsworth to characterize Manning:

> He was one in whom persuasion and belief had ripened
> into faith,
> And faith becomes a passionate intuition.

Here is what commitment to principle is all about: persuasion and belief maturing into faith, and faith becoming a conviction which is so strong and so passionate that it compels action within our world. And that's what the world needs—now!

Source Notes

Chapter 1

1. "From Fantasy to Reality," an interview with Malcolm Muggeridge, *Christianity Today,* April 21, 1978, p. 11.
2. For those who would like to read further on the development of synthesis within the framework of a Christian commitment, I suggest:

   Barcus, Nancy B., *Developing a Christian Mind* (Downers Grove: Inter-Varsity Press, 1977).

   Pike, Kenneth L., *With Heart and Mind* (Grand Rapids: Eerdmans, 1962).

   Schaeffer, Francis A., *The God Who Is There* (Downers Grove: Inter-Varsity Press, 1968).

Chapter 2

3. J. I. Packer, *Knowing God* (Downers Grove: Inter-Varsity Press, 1973) pp. 29, 30.

   See also: A. W. Tozer, *The Knowledge of the Holy* (New York: Harper and Brothers, 1961).
4. Bruno Bettelheim, *The Uses of Enchantment* (New York: Alfred A. Knopf, Borzoi Books, 1975), p. 10.

Chapter 3

5. Helmut Thielicke, "Why the Holocaust," *Christianity Today,* January 27, 1978, p. 9.

6. Leo Tolstoy, *Anna Karenina*, Constance Garnett, trans., (Indianapolis: The Bobbs-Merrill Company, 1978), p. 336.

CHAPTER 4

7. "A Face Aflame," interview with Annie Dillard, *Christianity Today*, May 5, 1978, p. 19.
8. William Shakespeare, *Hamlet*, 3.1. 78–80.
9. Solzhenitsyn, *Gulag*, p. 131.
   Some of the material in this chapter was published in *Eternity* under the title "Dark Passages." Used by permission.

CHAPTER 5

10. Rollo May, *The Courage to Create* (New York: W. W. Norton, 1975), p. 23.
11. Kenneth Hamilton, *To Turn From Idols* (Grand Rapids: Eerdmans, 1973), p. 95.
12. Edith Schaeffer, "Destructive or Constructive Freedom?" *Christianity Today*, May 5, 1978, p. 32.
13. W. E. Henley, "Invictus," in Untermeyer, *Treasury*, p. 985.
14. A. W. Tozer, *The Root of the Righteous* (Harrisburg: Christian Publications, 1955), p. 25.

CHAPTER 6

15. *See* my book *People in Process: The Preschool Years* (Old Tappan: Fleming H. Revell Co., 1978), pp. 59–65, for a fuller discussion of childhood commitment.
16. J. L. C., book review of the book *Mama Doesn't Live Here Anymore* in *Saturday Review/World*, June 1, 1974.
17. A fine contemporary example of the process of weighing the evidence and then making commitment is found in: Charles M. Colson, *Born Again* (Old Tappan: Fleming H. Revell Co., 1977), pp. 90–117.

See also:

C. S. Lewis, *Surprised by Joy* (London: Fontana Books, 1959).

C. S. Lewis, *Mere Christianity* (London: Fontana Books, 1952).

John R. W. Stott, *Basic Christianity* (Grand Rapids: Eerdmans, 1958).

CHAPTER 7

18. Sheldon Vanauken, *A Severe Mercy* (New York: Harper and Row, 1977), p. 98. A fuller text of the quotation is as follows: "The position was not, as I had been comfortably thinking all these months, merely a question of whether I was to accept the Messiah or not. It was a question of whether I was to accept Him—or *reject*. My God! There was a gap *behind* me, too. Perhaps the leap to acceptance was a horrifying gamble—but what of the leap to rejection?"

CHAPTER 8

19. Kirk Farnsworth, "The Myth of the Machine," *HIS Magazine*, February, 1974, p. 29. Reprinted by permission of the publisher.

20. For a discussion of the issues in the "baptism debate" with a view to promoting understanding, *see* Donald Bridges and David Phypers *The Water That Divides* (Downers Grove: Inter-Varsity Press, 1977).

John Claypool, in an interview reported in *The Wittenburg Door*, #42, April–May, 1978, pp. 6–22, suggests provocatively that early childhood commitment should be celebrated by inclusion at communion, with baptism reserved as a seal on adult commitment.

CHAPTER 9

21. Gail Sheehy, *Passages*, p. 215.

CHAPTER 10

22. Brian Moore, *The Luck of Ginger Coffey* (Toronto: McClelland and Stewart New Canadian Library, 1972), p. 243.

CHAPTER 11

23. Elton Trueblood, *The Company of the Committed* (New York: Harper and Row, 1961), p. 22.
24. James Olthuis, "Marriage," in *Baker's Dictionary of Christian Ethics* (Washington: Canon Press, 1973), p. 409.

CHAPTER 12

25. Margaret Mead, "Can the American Family Survive?" *Redbook*, February, 1977, p. 159.
26. Ellen Goodman, "Single-Minded Success—or Happy Families?" The *Boston Globe* Newspaper Company, 1978, reprinted in *The Guardian*.
27. Robert Thomas Allen, "Family is Belonging," *The Review*, Number 1, 1978, pp. 3–5.
    Some of the material in this chapter appeared in *Moody Monthly* under the title "Let Your Children Go!" Used by permission.

CHAPTER 13

28. John R. W. Stott, *Basic Christianity* (Grand Rapids: Eerdmans, 1958), pp. 141, 142.
29. John Donne, in Louis Untermeyer, *A Treasury of Great Poems* (Simon and Schuster, 1955), p. 355.
30. R. R. Lee, "I Found God in a Walk Across America," *Christian Herald*, September, 1979, p. 55.

CHAPTER 14

31. Victor G. Hopwood, ed., *David Thompson: Travels in Western North America, 1784–1812* (Toronto: Macmillan, 1971), p. 1.

32. Brother Lawrence, *The Practice of the Presence of God* (Old Tappan: Fleming H. Revell Co., 1953), p. 37.

33. John Oliver Nelson, *Work and Vocation: A Christian Discussion* (New York: Harper and Brothers, 1954), p. 108.

34. Elisabeth Elliott, *A Slow and Certain Light* (Waco: Word Books, 1973), p. 47.

35. A. W. Tozer, "The Sacrament of Living," in *The Pursuit of God* (Harrisburg: Christian Publications, 1948), p. 127.

CHAPTER 15

36. Jean Vanier, *In Weakness, Strength: The Spiritual Sources of General the Rt. Hon. Georges P. Vanier, 19th Governor-General of Canada* (Toronto: Griffin House), p. 59.

37. Thomas Griffith, "Party of One," *The Atlantic*, May, 1977, p. 26.

38. C. S. Lewis, *Mere Christianity*, p. 19.

39. John E. Smith, ed., *Works of Jonathan Edwards, Vol. 2: Religious Affections* (New Haven: Yale, 1959), p. 280.

40. Mark Hatfield, *Between a Rock and a Hard Place* (Waco: Word Books, 1976), p. 21.

41. Douglas Roche, *The Human Side of Politics* (Toronto: Clarke, Irwin, 1976), pp. 206, 209.